About the Author

I'm an award-winning essayist and journalist, appearing in national publications. I live with my husband and son in Connecticut.

Counterfeit Mother

Deborah DiSesa Hirsch

Counterfeit Mother

Olympia Publishers
London

www.olympiapublishers.com
OLYMPIA PAPERBACK EDITION

A CIP catalogue record for this title is
available from the British Library.

ISBN: 978-1-80439-341-3

This is a work of non-fiction.

First Published in 2023

Olympia Publishers
Tallis House
2 Tallis Street
London
EC4Y 0AB

Printed in Great Britain

Dedication

For Phillip.

Acknowledgements

Thank you, Phillip, for letting me use your life to tell our story.

God could not be everywhere, so he made mothers.

Prologue

A lot of people have wondered how I could expose my father for having abused me. I talk in the book about the ways I feel it affected my ability to get and stay pregnant, which ultimately led to my decision to use a donor.

Many in my family no longer talk to me, and that hurts. But this is my truth and I must share it to live my life fully, and be Phillip's best mother.

1

It feels strange to be wheeled through the old hospital, the dark paint peeling and pipes, cords and sharp metal pieces dangling from the open ceiling. It's like a ghost town. I can almost feel the souls who lived and died in these walls around me. I pray it's not an omen. I'm forty-seven and about to have my first baby.

"Are you ready?" Dr. Besser asks. "Your baby's almost here."

"Yes," I say. He looks happy after this long journey we've been on. But what I feel is fear. I don't know how to be a mother. He moves some instruments around and they make a clanging sound as they brush against each other. I don't want to see them because I know they are going to be cutting me open.

"You're going to feel some pressure," he says as he begins.

The surgery goes on for a long time. I'm trying not to think what it's going to be like having this baby, because he isn't going to feel like mine, and I kind of want to put it off, seeing him, for as long as I can.

I feel my husband, Larry, a dentist who never takes time off for anything, next to me, and he's nervous. My husband, who was raised in a family where no one spoke—or felt—their feelings, sits beside the bed like he's at a ball game. The only time he shows any emotion is when Phillip enters the world.

"He doesn't have my nose!" he cries.

Larry has always been self-conscious about what he calls his "Jewish" nose, which, along with his craggy features and good looks, is one of the things that immediately attracted me to him when I saw him in a crowded hallway at a singles' weekend in the Catskills, and smiled at him, feeling very bold. Now maybe Phillip will have them.

"He got the donor's nose," he exults, and I feel a little stab, not real but in my heart, something I will feel every time someone comments on their likeness.

He wants to watch the actual procedure but Dr. Besser says no, he doesn't want two patients.

The surgery goes on for a long time and I'm trying not to think what it's going to be like having this baby, because he isn't going to feel like mine, and I kind of want to put it off, seeing him, as long as I can.

"You're going to feel a little pressure," Dr. Besser says again, and I do, I can feel him pushing on my abdomen. I can't really feel anything else, no pain, just this pulling, and stretching of my stomach.

Finally, there's a cry, and a huge sob rises in my throat. A beautiful baby with no hair, just a shiny skull, is lifted towards me. He is here, and he is gorgeous.

This, this was what I waited for all these years, but I push it back down, embarrassed.

"Ten twenty-five a.m.," Dr. Besser pronounces.

I hate showing my feelings. And they are so raw. But this baby coming out of me doesn't feel like mine. As intimately as my body was used to house and grow, and now, deliver, this person, without another person's help, he would not be here. He does not come from me.

Some commotion is going on at the end of the table.

"Oh my God, you had twenty pounds of amniotic fluid," Dr. Besser says, then spills it on the floor. But I don't care. I have a baby, even if he doesn't feel like mine.

Now I understand why I only rarely felt Phillip moving inside me, leaving me to ask if I was doing something wrong. The five other pregnant women in my department all raved about how their babies were kicking and stretching and waking them up. I never felt any of this. Was it because I wasn't pregnant the "right" way? But the reality was, that he was swimming in so much amniotic fluid that I never so much as felt a splash. I think only I felt him kick once or twice.

Dr. Besser holds him up but I can't really see, I don't have my glasses on and there's equipment in the way. This way, I can put off the moment when I really get to look at him and not see my face in his.

Phillip's here for a minute. Larry gets to hold him, not me, not like in the commercials where they lay the baby on your chest. I barely have a glimpse of him with his bald head and blue, blue eyes. And then, he's whisked away.

Larry runs to the nursery to be with him but I have to remain behind while they sew me up. It takes forever. I'm starting to want to see the baby.

Finally, they wheel me to recovery, and Larry's there, but not Phillip. We have to stay there for about an hour. I ask Larry to call my parents.

"How big was he?" my mother asks. The doctors in the practice had placed bets on Phillip's size. Dr. Besser thought he'd be about eleven pounds but, "Eight pounds, fifteen ounces," Larry says. I'm disappointed and wonder if his biological mother had big babies, too.

Later, they bring Phillip to me for his first feeding. I'm a little scared to take him. What if I don't hold him right? But the nurse is very reassuring as she holds him out and I take him, this warm bundle of flesh that came out of my body, and I somehow know how to fold my hospital gown down and bring his head to my breast, and he latches on. I am feeding my child. I have never felt anything like this before. I have a baby. I don't think about who his mother is, I just hold him, and hope I can do it right.

2

I don't remember much else about the day Phillip's born, though I do, reluctantly, visit the nursery. I wonder if I can pick him out. All those baby faces.

I see him in the corner. He's bigger than the other babies. They have him dressed in what looks like a long-sleeved white T-shirt with a little flap over the heart, and there's a tiny cap with a blue label over his head. Baby Hirsch. Boy. Eight pounds, fifteen ounces. He has never felt more like the donor's baby. I wait for the rush of love. But I feel... nothing.

They keep bringing me this baby who now will not latch on. We have no choice but to switch to a bottle with formula—he has to eat. It's my first loss with him. When the baby cries, I ask the nurses to take him away. I can't help but wonder, would his biological mother have succeeded?

I even work with a lactation consultant. But still, no latching. Can he tell I'm not his real mother? I feel it again when I can't pump.

That night, the night after he was born, is a haze of painkillers and a crashing thunderstorm. Car alarms go off under my window, but I just want to sleep. Then, a nurse wakes me and asks if I've been tested for strep.

"I don't think so," I say, struggling to come up from the haze.

"Your baby's lips turned blue and he stopped breathing," she says. When I wake up, I wonder if it was a dream. The nurse who brings me breakfast says, in the kindest way possible, that Phillip might have to go to the neonatal intensive care unit. There's a problem with his heart.

I look at the sunny day outside, the light slicing through the trees, the new leaves ruffled by the breeze and the deep blue of the sky. Such peacefulness and calm, and I've just had my baby. This can't be happening.

My mother comes in and sits in the chair by my bed, with her musty scent and purse the size of a typewriter which bangs against my arm as she sits down. "How's the baby?"

I don't want to make it real so I don't say anything.

Larry arrives, tired from a day at work as a dentist in the city. We talk a little about the baby. But I have to be careful. He always thinks the worst and I can't handle it if he starts talking about burial and graveyards. He dives into the worst possible outcomes when the world is shaky.

I don't visit Phillip all day, though the nurses bring him to me for his bottle. I hold him but feel very far away. I am determined not to get too attached if he's going to die.

A young, single friend comes to visit. "So, what's his name?"

"Phillip Randle Hirsch," I say and it's the first time I feel a lick of ownership. "Randle" is my mother's maiden name.

That night, some more relatives come with a huge teddy bear and though I am glad to see them, I wish they would leave. It has been a long, troubling day.

Larry goes home, exhausted from his role as a father, though it hasn't really started yet. I remember taking a photo of him holding Phillip several hours after he was born and seeing the love flood his face, surprising both of us. This baby has always been my idea.

It becomes a game. Everyone is trying to figure out who he looks like. Thank God, he has the shape of Larry's head, his long, thin face, and bright blue eyes. My mother-in-law says he doesn't look like anyone. She says one of my most favorite things ever: "He looks like Phillip."

Yes, the baby is the spitting image of my husband—the same strong jaw, the deep blue eyes, the color of the ocean when the sun just hits it, the long, thin fingers, even at birth. Everyone will know he is the father.

Later that afternoon, almost as the sun is setting, the nurse comes to me with good news. The doctor has just circumcised the baby and he would not have done that if there was any chance Phillip wasn't going to be all right. It was a small hole in his heart, between the major vein and artery. It's not uncommon in newborns. The hole often closes by itself and it does. Thank God.

What I feel for this baby is love, certainly, love. But it's almost like I'm feeling it for someone else's child, a niece, or a nephew. And there is anger. Why can't I pop out babies like everyone else? I learn, over time, that I'm not alone. This is a common problem of mothers who have donor egg babies, feeling unable to attach.

Of the two million embryos to a woman's uterus recorded by the C.D.C. from 2000 to 2016, only 16,000 were donor embryos. But over that period, the annual number of donor transfers rose sharply -- from 334 in 2000 to 1,940 in 2016, according to the New York Times, and experts say it is continuing to increase. But over that period, the annual number of donor transfers rose sharply -- from 334 in 2000 to 1,940 in 2016, according to the New York Times, and experts say it is continuing to increase.

By the time a woman reaches 45, her chances of having a baby with her own eggs is about 2 percent, according to experts. But donor egg recipients with an average age of 42 can expect somewhere near a 51 percent chance of success. Using someone else's eggs is where the emotional part begins. I wonder if they all felt this way. I'll bet many did.

I know I have a long journey ahead of me.

3

I now have this beautiful baby who's such a good baby. He doesn't cry very much (I can call for the nurse when he does), he looks up at me (in the delivery room, a nurse tells Larry, "He's so alert. Look at him looking up at the ceiling"), and still I am feeling such isolation and sadness that I feel nothing for this baby.

The next day, (back then, you got four days in the hospital after a C-section) a friend comes and hands me a picture of Phillip in the nursery, the only one we have.

"I hear a lot of mothers don't connect with the baby right away," he says. What would he know, a single guy, with no kids? But it's what I'm thinking. He read my mind. How could I? A donor gave me this baby.

I visit the nursery again. I can pick him out by his size. He's big but he has no hair.

"Look at all that hair!" the technician said at my twenty-week ultrasound. And I had plenty of heartburn, an old wives' tale that the baby inside has a lot of hair. But, no hair. Still, he's beautiful.

The baby nurse we'd hired comes to pick me up. She looks surprised that Larry isn't picking me up. I dress Phillip in the fancy one-piece outfit I'd picked out, cute but not for taking a newborn home in, who knew? I struggle to fit him inside it. This is so hard, having a baby, having to know right away how to feed him and dress him, how to fit his arms and legs through the openings when he's squirming so much. Is it because I'm not his real mother that I don't know how to do this?

I realize, driving home with her, my eyes never leaving the precious back seat, terrified that something bad could happen, that if she didn't drive carefully or had to jam on her brakes, he could go flying. I now have a whole new way to fear.

I get Phillip out of the car seat and carry him carefully inside. I wish the baby nurse would have done it. But I manage, and we go inside. She instantly knows what to do. She takes him from me so I can put down the bag I have over my shoulder (who ever knew having a baby would be so complicated, one arm for holding him, another for grabbing your purse or your packages, still another for the car seat or pacifier, how do you do it all?) and then she moves gently back and forth on her feet so he probably feels as if he's still in the womb. How does she know how to do this?

She's not nervous at all. I am so jealous of the way she handles Phillip so confidently, knowing exactly how to cup his head and not feeling a flash of panic when he starts to cry. She simply rocks him and soothes him in a soft, lulling voice and he settles right down. How did she know how to do this so effortlessly? Would I ever learn? I'm thinking there's no one on earth less qualified to have a child.

4

When she leaves, I'm hit with a sudden, overwhelming rush of desperation to call her back. I don't know what to do. I've never had a baby before. How do I know what I'm doing is right? He's all my responsibility. This new life depends on me.

Don't most fathers go home with the babies and help the new moms, instead of leaving them to come home alone, terrified and almost hysterical? I go and put him in the crib and pray, pray, he won't stop breathing.

"What do I do if he does?" I asked the nurse at the hospital, hoping the panic wasn't showing in my voice.

"Call 911," she said, like, what *else* would you do?

I don't know, this is all so new to me, and he's not my baby.

The phone rings and it's Lenny, Larry's elderly aunt, calling from Florida.

"How are you? How's the new baby?"

"He's doing great," I say, knowing that if I tell her what happened with his heart, I will lose all control. So I tell her he has no hair but these big blue eyes. I try to keep talking about neutral things so I don't start crying, which is right at the bottom of my throat. They say new mothers get these feelings of depression and sadness from all the hormones floating around. I think in my case, it's because of everything that's happened trying to have this child.

"Well, give Larry my love and enjoy your new son," she says. We hang up and I'm thinking, now what? They can't leave me alone with this new baby.

I don't want Lenny to know how scared and desperate I feel. I'm completely responsible for this child for the rest of my life.

In the bedroom next door, he sleeps for a while and then wakes, crying. I hurry in and don't know what to do so I change him. His eyes close and he goes back to sleep. I take a breath. Maybe I can do this after all.

5

On the Sunday after Phillip was born, a friend brings dinner and I am heating it up when I feel a strange sensation and go to the bathroom. I am bleeding. I try to stop it using towels because toilet paper isn't thick enough to absorb it, but I can't.

I call the answering service and the covering doctor calls back right away and says, "Get to the hospital *now*." If I can't drive or don't have someone to take me, he'll send an ambulance. I am hemorrhaging.

I remember sitting in the back, holding Phillip, thinking, I can't die, I can't die. He's eight days old.

I look at this beautiful baby. I may not be his mother, but I can't leave him, not after just getting him. I pull the blanket around him. He should be in the car seat but I need to be able to touch and feel his warm soft, presence. Am I possibly thinking like a mother?

They take me right in and the nurses are waiting (people died from this, years ago) but everyone only has eyes for Phillip, sitting up in his car seat, looking around the ER. I want to hold him, feel his tiny chest rising against mine, not lie on this stretcher, connected to IVs

"He's adorable," says a nurse. I don't take any credit. How can I? His genes—and his looks—come from someone else.

The doctor comes to examine me. I will not die but I need surgery, dilation, and a curettage of the uterus, just like after my other two pregnancies. At least, this time, there is a baby. There are two cases ahead of me in the operating room, so I am going to have to wait a while. What are we going to do with the baby?

The last thing I want is to give him up, but he can't stay in the ER with me or with Larry all night. We call my sister but she doesn't want to have to deal with a newborn. So, we call the baby nurse and Larry takes Phillip to her house. I feel like a piece of my body has been taken away from me.

We don't know her that well, but we really don't have a choice. And then I wait and wait and wait for my surgery, thinking about Phillip and what happens if I don't make it, how would the donor feel?

I want to sing and dance. I just had a baby. But I'm confined to this room which smells like rubbing alcohol with an extra sack of saline on the counter behind me and an oxygen tank. Will I be needing that? I should be at a baby shower, eating a slice of cake with blue icing, and cradling my precious newborn. This is not what I expected.

Finally, around eleven p.m., they wheel me into the operating room where it's cold and bright. The surgeon tells me everything will go fine. I remember thinking, as the darkness pulls in: *Please, please, let me wake up. I just had a baby.*

6

I remember taking in as much air as I can, waking up. I'm alive! I just had surgery, I'm still here. I survived. I want to get up and rush to the baby nurse's house to get Phillip.

Larry walks beside the stretcher with the nurse, wheeling me to a room.

"We'd like you to stay the night," she says.

It's now close to two a.m. and I am so tired, that I just want to sleep.

"I can't pick you up in the morning," Larry says. "I have to go to work. You can take a taxi home."

But that's the last thing I want to have to think about so.

"No, I'm getting dressed," I say and somehow I do, though the only thing I want to do is put my head on that pillow and go to sleep.

"Are you ready?" Larry asks.

No, I want to say. I am still dizzy from the anesthesia. But I don't want to stay here. I want to get home and get my baby.

Finally, we are home and I go into the bathroom. It looks like a murder scene. There is blood everywhere. I get another towel, wet it, then begin wiping down the walls and the toilet seat, and the floor. Then, I go to lie down but I'm thinking, where's my baby? But I have to admit, I'm glad I don't have to get up when he cries and give him a bottle.

When the sun wakes me up, I realize, oh my God, I don't have my baby and I call the baby nurse right away. We didn't know her, didn't know if we could trust her, what were we thinking? He's only eight days old and she spent the night away from me. But Phillip is fine and she brings him home about an hour later.

I'm happy to see him, this cute little boy, and I take him into my arms right away. Even though I don't feel like his mother, I am glad he is home.

It's only now that it's becoming acceptable to admit to not loving being a mother. "How do you like motherhood?" a church friend asked when Phillip was a newborn. "I hate it."

I didn't say that but that's what I felt. I absolutely loathed the newborn stage, having to wake up multiple times to his crying (not for me, let him cry it out), then lying awake waiting for his next cry so I wouldn't be yanked from sleep, like someone turning on the lights when you've just dozed off and yelling, "Get up!" in your ear.

I hated how boring it was, sitting around all day, with the only highlight the changing of a diaper or feeding carrots with a tiny spoon that gets spit out at me.

I missed my career, even the insufferable executives who objected when we had to change "best ever" to "works well," in the press release.

This is what new mothers go through that no one tells you about.

Of course, there are the good times, like when he sees your face at the bus stop, or the dozens of cards, and the drawing pictures of us together, my favorite, the one showing him on the lawn and "my mother is in the window."

But motherhood is hard and sometimes torturous, and all we get for admitting that, even just to ourselves, is guilt.

Something has happened to Larry. Phillip has changed his life, even though he's only been here for a couple of weeks. For a man who has said "I love you" to me exactly once (and says, "Thank you," when I say it to him), he looks at his son with so much love in his eyes when he comes home, I can't believe it's the same man.

Something has happened to Larry. Phillip has changed his life, even though he's only been here for a couple of weeks. For a man who has said "I love you," to me exactly once (and says, "Thank you," when I say it to him), he looks at his son with so much love in his eyes when he comes home, I can't believe it's the same man.

A man who has always found it hard to show emotion or affection now lights up whenever Phillip is near him. The other morning, I heard him whispering into Phillip's ear, "I love you."

Why is it so easy for him to love Phillip, yet have so much trouble with me?

7

"C'mere," Larry says when he gets home and scoops Phillip into his arms, nuzzling his neck, pulling the curls out of his mouth. "What did we do before we had you?"

He looks for him the minute he comes home. If he's sleeping, he demands, "Where's Phillip?" He's holding him all the time. In fact, his mother asks, "Are you going to be holding him in college?"

I liked, at first, that he wasn't emotional or affectionate (no cards saying "I love you." In fact, any card he sent me would just be signed, "Me") or bought flowers for no reason. Or remembered our twenty-fifth anniversary. I liked that he never pushed me to have sex and left anything physical up to me. He's not big on presents—doesn't believe in celebrating birthdays or Christmas, which, true, is not his holiday. But a hand reaching for mine, or an arm around me in a movie theater made me start to feel like something was missing.

Larry's love is quiet. He tries to get me to eat more vegetables. He implores me to swim and not run when my knee is hurting. And he never wanted the dog but he says he loves how his tail wags when I pet him because it means he loves me. He also stays up with him at night for his 1 a.m. trip outside.

Actually, to be fair, I hated the boyfriends who sent me cards signed "love," or worse, "love, always." Somehow, it reminded me of my father. I always thought I was missing something with Larry's way of showing love. But with Phillip, I now understand.

It's all there in his heart. It's just very hard for him to show it.

One night, Larry tells me he looked at Phillip and saw God. This from the man who, the only time he set foot in a synagogue for Phillip's bar mitzvah.

Now, months later, I get it. Love flows so easily, so effortlessly for this child. I have to work for it with Larry. But it all comes so naturally, so automatically, with this child, no matter whose he is.

The night your dad and I met, in a dark bar, I could see how authentic he was. He didn't play games, he spoke straight from the heart about whatever we were talking about, not caring if I thought his need to keep checking for his room key in his pocket was odd.

"I always lose things," he told me apologetically. "I'm a total mess at keeping track of my stuff."

I was touched by his vulnerability when he barely knew me. I knew right away that this was someone I could spend my life with.

One autumn weekend, he and I decide to go up to the Berkshires to a hotel, formerly a huge mansion, with a big wraparound porch and views of the mountains. It's early autumn and the trees are a blast of red and yellow. We hike up one of the less challenging hills and admire the gorgeous view, mostly other hills and lots of trees. We go for lunch, then back to the room, a spartan arrangement of twin beds under scratchy wool blankets, a strip of indoor-outdoor carpet, and a windowless bathroom.

Outside, kids scream and laugh, playing on the jungle gym. The light is bright, shining through the leaves and picking out the dust motes on the blankets.

"Now what should we do?" Larry asks. He glances toward the twin beds. I know what he's thinking. But I have always been the one to initiate sex.

"I guess," I say and turn the blanket back. I don't want to have sex. All I can think about is how scratchy and uncomfortable the blanket will be and how soon we can be done.

We have sex when I want to and he goes along with that. He had a pretty strong sex drive when we met. Like all things, you can get too comfortable, and now we only have relations when I want to. Later, I will realize that having control over sex is related to my incest.

The rest of the day is normal. We take another walk and watch the setting sun, then go to dinner in the big cafeteria-style restaurant. It's noisy and loud.

"What can I get for you?" the waiter asks.

"Broiled chicken," I say.

"And as your side?"

"Broccoli."

It's not at all what I want but I have to lose weight to fit into my bridesmaid's dress for my sister's wedding in two weeks.

Larry orders the steak. When it arrives, thick and sizzling, with French-fried onion rings, I have to look away. My chicken is dry.

We talk about the day, and what's coming up next week. I don't say anything about this strange way I am feeling. I'm scared of it.

"What would you like for dessert?" the waiter asks as he takes the plates away.

"Nothing for me," I say.

"Death by chocolate," Larry says, and I have to watch him dig into all that melting chocolate and ice cream and focus on my hot tea. For a treat, I put cream in. I'm looking for the comfort that eating that would give me, and I can't have it.

8

Even though I never had a weight problem, I always thought I did. I had an eating disorder for a while in high school and food was my one source of comfort. When I was eating, everything else fell away.

The desperation for this dessert was the first stirrings, dark and disturbing, of what was coming. This is when the feelings started about the place in your body where you have a baby.

It's only a few days later that this funny feeling is something I can't get rid of. I'm driving and my hands are shaking on the wheel. My heart feels like it could jump out of my chest. My breath is coming in short puffs. I'm scared it may stop. I'm having my first panic attack.

As I keep driving, my throat feels like it is closing. It's getting harder to breathe. I don't know what this is at all but I'm frightened. I'm starting to get my body memories back, but I don't know this yet.

I don't know how to explain the tightness in my chest or this very unpleasant feeling between my legs. I don't know what it is and I don't like it. What's worse, I don't know how to stop it. I've always been able to handle just about anything with my body, falls and broken ankles and wrists, a wound requiring eight stitches over my eye from a running accident, crampy and very painful periods. But not this.

I feel very weird. The days go on. I go to work and come home and make dinner but something very dark is hanging over me. I don't tell Larry.

He knows I was molested, I told him early on, when we met. But I'm not connecting it all yet. It seemed an important thing that he needed to know about me. I can't bring myself to talk about this new feeling. One night, I just tell him I'm going out, and I get in the car and drive to the beach, then pull over and scream in the car. I wonder what people might think.

Do they see me with my mouth open and my face twisted in anguish? They can't hear me but does my face tell the story? My throat feels like it's closing, and I find that, when I eat, I sometimes can't swallow and am terrified I will choke so I chew everything up into tiny pieces. No one can hear me; the windows are rolled up. I find I need to do it every couple of days. I don't tell Larry.

The feelings continue. One night in the car at the beach, watching the waves curl onto the pebbly shore, I realize, I'm having a panic attack. Naming it helps a little, then makes me feel worse. I don't want to be having a panic attack. But it's here and I can't seem to take a breath. What if I stop breathing? It seems possible.

"Breathe," I tell myself. "Breathe." I take one deep breath, and then another. I'm able to drive home and get through the rest of the night. But I still don't tell Larry.

Another night, I'm driving through Stamford, and I come to the Arthur Murray dance studio. I can see, through the windows, people having fun, twirling and swinging as they hold hands. It makes me realize that somewhere, somehow, people are having fun. There is happiness in the world, not all darkness and desperation. Maybe, one day, I will have it, too.

9

It all comes to a head with my family when Larry and I decide to get married and I call to tell my parents. We've been dating for ten years and it was always expected but there's something about telling them that's making me feel surprisingly nervous. We've not spoken for several years, as I'm working through my own issues around abuse.

"We're getting married," I say and immediately feel disloyal to my father.

"When?" my mother says, sounding a little surprised.

I'm reminded of her always forcing me to do things with my father. When I was in high school, she constantly suggested we went to dinner and a movie, just the two of us.

"Where would you like to eat?" my father asked.

"You choose," I said, so he picked an upscale restaurant the family never went to, with white tablecloths and linen napkins. When the waiter comes for our order, my father said, "Why don't you ask my wife?"

About my wedding, I tell my mother, "In May. At the Homestead in Greenwich." I'm picturing lots of flowers and sitting outside at this elegant old hotel and restaurant. "Do you want to come wedding dress shopping with me?"

"Yes!" she says.

I drive us to Westport (she won't drive on I-95) and talk about the kind of wedding I want to have. "

Probably May or June. In a garden somewhere. Lots of

ribbons and flowers," I dream out loud.

When we get to the store sadly, most of the dresses are in 's' tiny sizes. I find one I really like, Victorian, with long lace sleeves and a high neck, but it just won't fit. I come out to show her and she pretends to show interest, but I know she's counting the minutes until lunch and her Manhattan.

We have just been served our water and her Manhattan, and are looking at the menu, when, out of nowhere, she says, "Did your grandfather molest you?" It's right after I say I won't have my father walk me down the aisle.

It's the first time it's ever been brought up in my whole life.

"No," I say. "Daddy did." My grandfather, her father, told me I had nice legs when I was in fifth grade.

My mother and I had a complicated relationship. From an early age, I was told by my father that she had been molested as a child and so we had to make special exceptions for her. We shouldn't be angry or disappointed if a kid bullied us on the bus and she acted like she couldn't be bothered to deal with it, or be excited about me being asked to the prom. And then it dawns on me. I have no idea how to be a mother because I have never had one.

When I get home, I have a message waiting for me. My father has called and he is spitting, he's so angry. She told him. He denies it, of course, and that's the end of my relationship with them.

10

It's a quiet Saturday and I'm on my way to Danbury to go wedding dress shopping again. I'm with an old friend who just got separated so it's not exactly a time either of us is looking forward to. Besides, Danbury is an old factory town, they used to make hats here, but it's hardly the height of fashion. I look through dresses and nothing jumps out at me. A saleswoman asks if she can bring some dresses in.

"Yes," I say, "Sure." But I'm feeling this strange nudge of dread.

Getting married was something I always thought I wanted to do. Now my real feelings are coming through. I've always had a problem with commitment. That's why, I guess, I chose men who were not available and was terrified of those who were.

In college, a boyfriend asked me, on the sorority phone, "How do you feel about marriage?"

"I guess," I answered gaily, "It would depend on who was asking me." I wonder now if that was a proposal or a prelude to one. But there was no way I could marry this man, my life too marked by uncertainty and loss, and this is what felt safe.

Did I pursue Larry so relentlessly because I couldn't have him and then, when I could, I didn't?

I remember how uneasy I felt when Larry went to switch his New York driver's license to a Connecticut one. Permanence. Maybe that's one of the reasons it took me so long to know I wanted children. I finally learnt about commitment when I become pregnant with you.

All these years, I blamed Larry for not wanting to get married but now this wedding is pulling up feelings I didn't know I had. Am I the one who didn't want this all along?

"How about this?" The saleslady brings in a dress with a huge bow at the back, the style at the time. I hate it but it fits, and I decide to buy it. I don't feel the satisfaction I thought I would. It was relatively cheap, only a couple of hundred dollars (the whole wedding is on me), so I give her my credit card and I have a dress.

We go out to lunch and my friend mostly talks about her separation. "Can you believe he told me he's no longer in love with me?" Tears shine in her eyes.

"I can't think of anything worse," I say, and it's true. If Larry ever said that to me, it would finish it. Then she brings up the wedding.

"I don't think I can read what I was going to," she says. "It's about love and patience and I just can't do it now."

I feel a little annoyed, but I understand how hard this must be for her—me starting a new life and hers ending. I want to tell her we're really not in such different situations. I love Larry but I'm afraid of it. And her husband just put it into words.

I continue with all the wedding preparations, flowers and cake, and plates and napkins and glasses and a small buffet dinner (ironically, the woman who arranged this also arranged your christening). But you weren't even a thought in my mind. I could no more think of having a child than of enjoying the wedding ceremony.

I feel this same dread when I pick out the flowers, and when the florist comes to our condo on the day of the wedding to arrange them.

11

The wedding I have been hoping for does not happen. Larry and I get married less than three months later, at our condo, on a gloomy winter day, with snow hanging heavy in the sky, with just his family and two of my closest friends. I come down our stairs in a wedding dress with a friend playing the flute in the background. A justice of the peace reads the vows. Larry steps on a lightbulb (glasses don't shatter easily) and that's it.

Looking at the JP, and thinking, am I really doing this? Am I really getting married? And without my family? Somehow, it doesn't feel real. I've never done anything permanently, for life, and this is making me very uncomfortable. I have none of the joyous feelings most people have on their wedding day. After all this time, am I the one who really didn't want to do this?

I go to the hardware store the next day to buy something for storing the top layer of the cake in the freezer. This is what you're supposed to do, I've been told, until your first anniversary when you eat it. I feel the same anxiety placing it in the container and putting it in the freezer.

I didn't invite anyone from my family, a little afraid of what my brother might do, and this is something I regret to this day. But that was the way it happened.

I decide to confront my father at a diner near my apartment.

Orders are shouted over the counter into the kitchen, dishes crash against each other and waiters rush around, slinging plates

41

of eggs and fried chicken and spanakopita and I feel like I'm in the middle of a raging tropical storm. Two cops sit at the counter, coffee cups in hand, eating slices of blueberry pie. Just a normal day for them.

"So, what do you think happened?" he asks.

"I know what happened," I say though I can't bring myself to say the words, you touched me.

I don't believe there was ever penetration, but there is enough body memory to know something happened, and looking at him makes me feel queasy. Am I actually remembering this right? Did he really do it? Looking at him, I see my father, a man I love, a judge, and a state legislator, but someone I can't look at without feeling squeamish. And a little nauseous. Could I have been *wrong*?

We've resolved nothing and we know it. I get up to leave, thinking, should I kiss him. But that's the old me and I don't have to do this anymore.

You weren't even a twinkle in my eye at this meeting, but I know one thing. I am never ever leaving you alone with my father.

12

Getting pregnant didn't take away what happened, but it sweetened the part of me that had been destroyed. When I became pregnant, this space in my body that had felt always rotted and spoiled became filled with light and a sense of hope.

All of a sudden, my body is holding a thing of beauty, not something that had turned my uterus into a dark cave.

For a long time, after making love, I cried. I sometimes wonder what my relationships would have been like without my father. But he's always been there, in the shadows.

13

Sex only became enjoyable to me with my first serious boyfriend, a man separated from his wife. I put his ability down to being married. But it's not that. He just knows how to please a woman and we have sex everywhere, in his car at a church where his wife is attending a service, on top of a bureau on vacation, in the front yard of the home he grew up in.

He's eight years older than me and a father of two, one a newborn. Sex becomes something to look forward to, not dreaded or feared. It's like he's wiped out all the uncomfortable, confusing feelings that I've had all these years. Years later, I come to understand that there was a sexual thrill between his being a father, and my father and that sex had always been part of my relationship with my father, even though I didn't consciously know it.

The fact of having little or no memories made me think they weren't real for a very long time. But I always had the body memories and, in becoming pregnant, something else is now in that dank, raw space.

I have no doubt that my shame about not being entitled to feel like Phillip's mother comes from this shame. Aunts, uncles, and cousins all stopped talking to me. The guilt was so bad that I carried it for many years.

My siblings stopped talking to me. I thought my godmother, who was my mother's best friend and father's first cousin, would be the first to comfort me. But everyone stopped talking to me.

The shame was the killer.

The somewhat interesting thing is that I never worried about the embryos being implanted in my uterus, even when one became Phillip. The idea of inserting an embryo into that cavern of darkness somehow didn't make me feel squeamish. It was separate from me. It wasn't mine. But it could become mine. Even then, I knew that.

After we're married, I don't think about getting pregnant right away. I knew from the start it would be hard for me to get pregnant but I hadn't thought anything about using a donor. I was still hoping against hope that I could get pregnant with my own eggs, as unlikely as it was at forty-two, my age when I started trying.

I decide to see a fertility specialist. We have our first conversation when I'm at the seashore for a couple of days. Larry couldn't get away. I start reading everything I can get my hands on, do the ovulation thing, keep my legs straight up in the air for a half-hour after intercourse and use egg whites instead of moisturizer, but nothing is working.

The seagulls are squawking and the waves are crashing. I'm on the pay phone and the sand is crunchy between my toes.

"Your hormone levels are very good," Dr. Lavy says. "We'll start with inseminations."

"No IVF?" I say, so relieved we won't have to start there. Sand scrunches like sugar between my toes.

"No, you shouldn't need it," he says. "I believe you will get pregnant this way."

We decide to start next month and though my heart is pounding and I'm feeling a little fear, there's a boat splashing through the shimmering waves, ruffling like lace around it, and the sheer beauty of it makes me hopeful that I can do this.

I go through four inseminations ("This time, you will get pregnant," says Dr. Lavy, after the fourth). I clench a little inside. Am I still not ready? But I don't get pregnant.

Dr. Lavy finally suggests IVF and reluctantly, I agree. I take all the hormones (hiring a nurse to give me the shots because Larry's too squeamish) and go for the retrieval of my eggs. I'm surprised that I have eight. Six fertilize but I don't get pregnant.

14

I do another IVF in October. I'm nearing the end of the cycle when the ultrasound shows only one egg.

"We can't do it with just one egg," the nurse says. "We'll do an insemination."

We all know it's a waste of time but I do it anyway.

In November, Dr. Lavy suggests another consultation and I know it's time to start discussing using a donor egg.

I've been feeling a little sick, with stomach problems but I've always had a nervous stomach. I think of canceling, then decide to go.

Sitting down in Dr. Lavy's office, I remember the last time I was in here, with such hope, two years ago, when we started out. All his degrees and his positions on the reproductive medicine staff at Yale line the wall. But he couldn't help me.

"So, we've been trying for a while," Dr. Lavy starts. "Is working with a donor something you would consider?"

I look at Larry. He's bored. This whole baby-making venture is my idea and he's not sure he's that into it. Plus, he's really afraid of the risk of a donor.

"What if the baby has Down Syndrome? Or flunks out of school?" he's asked me. I've thought of this, too, of getting a girl pregnant or having to rush to the emergency room because he's overdosed.

"It will be ok," I say, but, of course, I don't really know this.

What none of us knows is that I am pregnant, at that moment.

I remember I waited two weeks until I ovulated, and the insemination was done. Then I forgot about it. It's so unlikely that I could be pregnant.

It's right before Christmas. We're having dinner at a pizza joint in our neighborhood. Strange things are happening in my body. I had noticed at work that my breasts hurt. And I haven't had a period in over a month, though that's not unusual, after an IVF cycle. But... I take a chance and say it.

"There's a chance I'm pregnant. I'm so excited!"

Larry reaches across the table for my hand. "Let's just take it a step at a time." He's holding something back, I can tell. It's that he knows, and I, in all my hysteria and joy, don't know that being pregnant doesn't always mean staying pregnant.

I can't take the test until the morning and I barely sleep all night. I remember waking up around five a.m. and being afraid to take it. I wait as long as I can, then go into the bathroom. The second line appears almost immediately. Pregnant. No having to wait the three minutes, like the test says.

"Larry, I'm pregnant!" I yell and dash back into the bedroom. He wants to look happy but I can see the fear on his face.

The nurse at Dr. Lavy's cautions me not to get too excited. They have to check my hormones to see the likelihood of my pregnancy continuing to a "live birth" (words I've never heard before).

I try to convince myself not to get too excited. My hormone levels are not where they should be. But it's early. I spend the day not quite believing that I am going to have a baby, while at the same time, tamping down the words of the nurse that we have a long way to go.

15

During the next week, I have a series of blood tests and though certain levels are still low, everything seems to be on track.

The day we go to hear the heartbeat, I am so excited I can't sit still in the waiting room. When they call us in, I jump up. They scan my uterus, looking for the little beating light on the screen. There isn't one.

I am numb. Even though they had told me this might happen, I just can't believe it. I drive to Stop & Shop, buy the mini cupcakes with all the frosting, and scrape the icing off the top with my tongue. It feels so good going down, but then I feel sick. It hasn't helped at all.

I don't miscarry on my own, so I have to have a D&C two days before Christmas. I remember feeling very sorry for myself. To find out I was pregnant, and in this way, so unexpectedly, and now this. I'm feeling very sorry for myself until the nurse taking care of me tells me that she lost her son at ten when he was hit by a car while riding his bike.

I get pregnant one more time, with my own eggs, just after we buy a house and six months after my first pregnancy. New house, new baby, a friend says.

I go through the two weeks after transfer calmly. I've been here before. When it comes time for the ultrasound, I'm a little apprehensive. Larry couldn't come so I sit in the waiting room, reading about one of his favorite tennis stars and some disaster that befell him, not knowing mine is coming up. I'm keenly alert of my name being called. This time, I walk in more cautiously and get up on the table with some fear.

They insert the probe and my uterus comes up on the screen. Once again, there is a black space with a small white object in the corner. There is nothing flashing, to indicate a heartbeat. How can I get and stay pregnant when I'm rotted inside from the abuse?

"I'm sorry," Dr. Lavy says.

He leaves and I get down off the table, my heart beating wildly. While I can't say I am surprised, I'm devastated. I have to spend the whole day carrying it around inside me like a piece of rotting fruit because I can't reach Larry.

He comes home early and I remember lying on the bed with him, watching the very last episode of my favorite soap opera, "Another World" (the main character had just found out she was pregnant with twins). True, they were just a clump of cells. But to us, they were a baby. I feel like everything is ending.

16

This is a hard time for us. He's still not sure he wants to become a parent. I think he's secretly glad my pregnancies didn't work out. It's summer, not the dark days of December, after my first failed pregnancy. But the light and warm temperatures don't really help. I move around the house, go to work, and try to do my errands, but I am so depressed that it's hard to keep going.

Then there's this Sunday in August. In just a few days, I will have my second D&C for this second failed pregnancy. It sits like a brick in my stomach. My uncle, my father's best friend, has invited me to have lunch at his yacht club after church. Here we are, sitting in this atmosphere of wealth and good fortune, looking at all the beautiful blond families.

This has turned me into a bitter person. Am I too bitter to love a baby?

I come in with my insides clenched. Am I going to have to defend myself again? It's nice, though, I have to admit, sitting with people who are talking quietly and politely to their families, seeing the water ripple out the window, about to have a nice lunch, and clinking glasses as someone does a toast. No crisis anywhere. It's all very normal, the most normal thing I've done in over a year. It's the first time I've been with a family member and not felt blame or fear.

The air conditioning hums comfortingly in the background. There's the slap of menus on tables, conversations in soft voices, and forks clinking on salad plates. Even though I know my uncle is not there to hurt me, it's what I expect from my family. I take a deep breath and get ready.

But I don't bring it up, and neither does he, my father's abuse, though I suspect he suspects, and that that is really what this lunch is about. He believes me and is silently offering his support. We talk quietly about his kids (I was his daughter's maid-of-honor) and what the grandkids are up to. I feel my pregnancy loss again. I'm the only one in all these families without a child.

Finally, in the end, we hug and go to our cars. When I get in the house, Larry is standing at the door, his face white. "Where *were* you?"

"I was having lunch with Uncle Ralph at his club."

"Why didn't you call me?"

It's kind of weird because we don't keep tabs on each other.

"I don't know," I say. "I just went with him after church." In those days, there were no cell phones.

"I went to church and I was able to get in but no one was there and I went out to the playground and then the door locked and I couldn't get back out." It's not until he's at the end of this frantic and embarrassing event, that I figure that's why he's so upset. "I thought you might be having a miscarriage."

It's the first time I realize that, despite his inability to express his feelings, he loves me.

17

Dr. Lavy has a notebook full of women who have agreed to be donors. I flip through the pages and nothing really grabs me until I come to one who is part Cuban, part French. She might have my dark hair. She already has two children, a boy, and a girl, who would be Phillip's half-siblings, and she works as a police dispatcher about forty miles away.

She's a little overweight (like me) and wears glasses (also, like me) but I really don't like that she's a smoker and wonder if that's why she hasn't been chosen by other women.

I agree to move forward with her. It's May. But I'm not really ready and am glad to learn that her birth control is in place for three more months and we have to wait till the end of the summer to align our periods, the beginning of our effort to produce a child.

We plan for the egg removal and transfer to be in September. In the meantime, Larry's mother has arranged a trip to Maine to see her family so we drive up there. It's a pleasant trip, we go out to several nice restaurants and a famous beach. His cousins all have children and oddly, I'm not bothered by this. The donor is in the back of my mind.

When we come back, I go to lunch with my friend, Laura, who thinks I'm a little nuts for taking this route, as do most people. We are in a diner, dishes clashing, men with yellow ties speaking over other men with yellow ties (those were the days when yellow meant power), the sun splashing over us.

"Are you really sure you want to do this?" she asks. "What if she takes drugs? Or is bipolar?"

"You're right, I don't know." I feel a little stab of fear. There's so much we won't ever know.

Realizing all the things that could go wrong still doesn't stop me from pushing on. I know there are lots of issues I can't control—we'd get a family health history from the donor but who knew how accurate it would be? Will she stop smoking while taking the drugs? If she doesn't, will that hurt the baby?

Finally, the day is here. Eleven eggs, nine fertilized. I have nine chances. But I only need one. On the report they give us, they look pretty good, all round circles with what look like bubbles inside them. I have no idea what I should be looking for. They just look like circles to me. Is our baby in there?

Three eggs are transplanted. I won't know for two weeks. At times, I think I'm pregnant. At others, I don't. I don't know what I will do if I fail again.

The time goes very slowly. I buy myself flowers so I have something beautiful to look at. I get up and go to work and joke around with my office mate, a young Russian man I've become very close to, who becomes very protective, once I tell him I'm pregnant (I was sharing the same office with him after my second failed pregnancy).

"You seem like something is wrong," he said.

But I couldn't tell him. I've been pregnant three times since I started sharing this office with him.

18

The time drags. But the day arrives.

The way it works is the office calls you on day fourteen to tell you whether you're pregnant. All the other times, the calls have started with, "I don't have good news for you."

I almost don't pick up when I see the light flashing. It's the nurse, Cindy, who works with the donor patients.

"I have good news for you," she says. "You're pregnant!"

Of course, I've heard that before. But this time she says, "Your HCG level is seven hundred. That's phenomenal." I remember it was under one hundred the other times.

"Am I having twins?" I say excitedly.

"No. Just a very healthy baby."

I run into a friend's office and tell her, and she hugs me. She was with me through my two failures.

"You're going to be a mother, after all," she says.

Will there be parts of you I will not recognize? Genes, of course, play a huge role, and part of you—no, half—of you will be something we will never know. Of course, no one knows who their child will be. But it's more complicated for us. Part of you will always be a mystery to us.

This child I nourished with my body will always have a side of him I don't know. But I don't want to get too ahead of myself. I've been pregnant before.

And then it's the day they check for the heartbeat. It will be the third time that I wait to hear a heartbeat. I have a heavy heart myself, in anticipation. I'm a nervous wreck, going to the bathroom every five minutes, looking out the window for Larry, who went out to exercise. I can't think of doing anything other than praying for a baby.

There shouldn't be much to worry about as all my hormone levels are exactly where they should be. But I can't shake off those two other horrible visits when there was no heartbeat.

I get up on the table and slip my legs into the stirrups. I hate this part, but not if it's going to show me my baby.

Dr. Lavy inserts the instrument.

I wait for the flat, white speck on the ultrasound. And there it is. A beautiful, beating heart, flashing on the screen.

A baby is coming.

"Isn't it amazing?" the nurse says. "That heart will beat for seventy years."

At that moment, I don't think, whose baby is this? I know, at least right now, it is mine.

The pregnancy goes very well after the first couple of weeks, during which I was sure I was going to lose it. I even pee on a pregnancy stick again to see that I am pregnant. At about week ten, I go into the bathroom and I'm bleeding. This can't be happening. I call the doctor's office in a panic.

The nurse on the phone is comforting. "We very rarely lose a pregnancy after we see a heartbeat. But if you want to come in for an ultrasound, you can."

I'm working from home that day so I jump in the car and race downtown. I get up on the table and they work the wand around inside me and that heart is still beating like crazy.

"See? I told you," the nurse says. "Sometimes your body doesn't know you're pregnant and you might start to have a period." They said to call if the bleeding gets worse, but, thankfully, it stops.

I wound up gaining fifty pounds (I felt better finding out twenty of it was amniotic fluid), and as my pregnancy progresses, I begin to believe that maybe, just maybe, there might be a baby.

19

The doctors decide to take Phillip a week early. A nursing friend told me it was because I'm a "multigravida," which means an older mother. That's better than a "geriatric pregnancy," which they also call us. It's also because he's very big.

And then, there's Phillip!

On one of our first office visits, I take his onesie off and the tip of his umbilical cord falls on the floor. My last physical connection to him.

I'm in group therapy two weeks after Phillip is born. This topic comes up a lot, my not feeling like Phillip's mother. It's a beautiful summer night and the crickets are making a racket in this North Stamford backyard. As it starts to get dark, it's my turn to speak.

"I don't feel like his mother," I say.

A man I don't know very well speaks up. "Your blood ran through him. You gave him life," he says.

He can see that I'm not convinced. "If someone gave you a kidney, would you feel it wasn't yours?" he asks.

I think about it.

There's no one who will have my weird eyes, sometimes brown and sometimes green in the right light. You'll never develop my grandpa's pitching arm, or my grandmother's ability to play the piano (she was a concert pianist in London). But you're you and that's the point.

In these early days, I tiptoe in and look at you in the crib.

There's a baby in this house, and he's supposedly mine. Despite the sadness I'm still feeling that you aren't really my baby, I'm also starting to feel some affection for you. You're curled up on your stomach, your little bottom high up in the air, something you're not supposed to let them do because of crib death, especially with your breathing problem. But I don't want to wake you to turn you over. You're sleeping, and I don't dare do anything to wake you and then have to make another decision about what to do with you.

For a minute, looking at this tiny, vulnerable human, I want to feel more than him being just an intruder in my home.

Why do I think I deserve this baby? What makes me entitled to him? I realize this is the abuse talking and yet the tape plays every time I look at this beautiful boy.

Is this how other mothers feel? If he had come from me, would he still feel so foreign? He is tiny and vulnerable and I have to care for him. But as for motherly instinct, I don't feel it. I had thought it would come with his birth, but as much as I care for him, I just don't feel like his mother.

His little body is curled up on my running shorts. They say to give newborns something that has your scent. Maybe I'm not feeling like his mother but there is this intense, violent instinct to keep this baby near me. I feel desperate when my mother-in-law suggests that Larry and I come to her Long Island club for dinner, and try to make us not have to go. I feel panic when I have to go to Greenwich, just one town over. I need to stay in Stamford, near this baby.

I pull his bassinet up next to my bed, his body next to mine. I don't really understand it, but I have this desperate need to hold him, to be next to him, keeping that soft warm body where I can see him and touch him and make sure he's breathing. Maybe it's the maternal instinct that kicks in every time a woman is near a baby. It's happened for thousands of years, no matter how you may deny it or think you don't feel it.

Every time I look at him, though, it makes me sad that what I mostly think about right now are his physical parts, what needs to be wiped or wrapped or fed, not this unswerving love for him. I care about him, I certainly do. He's a defenseless little baby. I'm starting to think that some of this comes from my own mother, who didn't know how to be a mother. I'm just not sure I feel that instinctual pull.

Sometimes, when I lay him on my chest, it feels right. I don't think about who's his real mother. I smell his head, his sweet baby smell, milky and a little sour. I feel him, he is real in my arms and want him any way I can have him. Holding his heart to my heart, his solid, warm weight and his soft breathing make me glad for all the horrible things that happened in trying to have a baby.

20

I try several more times to get him to latch onto my breast and he won't. It takes away from the feeling of peace holding him sometimes gives me. So, it's on to formula. I heat the bottle in the microwave, change him every couple of hours and check to make sure his chest is still rising. I even get up three or four times at night, just to make sure. I'm just doing what's right, not like a mother. At least, it doesn't feel like that. I want him to be more than work and fatigue.

As soon as I start to do the wash, he's crying and I have to run in to see, now what? Is he hungry? Does he need to be changed? *Why* is he crying?

Larry isn't around, not coming home till late, sometimes after eight o'clock, when I feel I've reached my breaking point. Why did I have this baby, anyway? What if I can't figure it out and something is really wrong? And where is someone who can tell me if I'm doing it right? It's certainly not my mother. Would his real mother know? Wait. I have to stop calling her that. But I still think about it all the time. Is she a good mom? Are there other half-siblings out there? She has two other children. She's in her early thirties as we do this. Does she work with other families? Does she ever wonder about the babies she helped to make? I don't really want to know all this. But just as he is part of her, she is part of him.

I wonder sometimes about your half-brother and sister. Are they as athletic as you? Do they have your aptitude for math? (In

61

your second year of college, you place in the top 2.8 percent of students in applied math at your university). I flunked geometry and algebra and just about everything else. But your father's mother was supposedly good with numbers and a genius at bridge so it probably came from her.

Do either of your co-siblings lose their front teeth at three, and have a huge, gaping hole in their mouth until they were six? Do they hate to be put in a playpen and scream until they are let out?

Do they have a special object that they love, and need to carry all of the time, like your tiny pillow in the soft blue flannel pillowcase? One time, out running with you in the stroller, you must have dropped it because when we get home, no pillow. I panic. How will I get you to sleep without it? I sometimes think your babysitter Nancy loves you even more than I do. She sews you two new flannel pillowcases; in case we lose it again. I still have one in my closet.

"How could you not know he dropped it?" Nancy exclaims when she comes over, later in the day. "It's his most precious possession."

It's true, this pillow and its soft flannel pillowcase, which I bought when you were sick, has become what you go to for comfort. You carry it everywhere, when we go out to eat, to visit Aunt Debbie (we had to race thirty miles back to get it), and especially when you go to sleep at night. You cannot sleep without it. How am I going to get you to sleep tonight?

"I can't believe you did that," Nancy says. "You have to keep your eye on it every minute, something so precious to him. What were you thinking? What kind of mother are you?"

"I didn't know, I dropped it," I say and she just gives me that frown that she always wears when I do what a mother who doesn't know anything would do. She wears it a lot.

"I'll just make him a new one," she says, smugly. And she did, she went out and got the flannel and whipped it up on her sewing machine. This is why I put up with her.

But the next day, there it is, in the road, and a bit dirty. I'll just wash it.

21

And what if I saw your biological mother? Would I see your face in hers? It's true, you're a miniature version of Daddy. But there has to be some of her in you. Sometimes I wonder if I met your bio mother, would I immediately like her? Do you get your kind and caring ways from her?

So many things from when you were a baby. The day I was bathing you and noticed your ribs moving up and down rapidly, and realized you can't breathe. I rushed you to the pediatrician, who diagnosed asthma and put you on prednisone, something they put you on every time this happened, only for me to discover that babies can't be on this medicine more than once a year. It made you jumpy and crabby and when we went out to eat, I remember having to walk you home (the restaurant was very close, one reason we picked it), because you couldn't sit still.

I'm remembering the nights you were struggling to breathe, and I would panic but have to keep my wits around me to keep you breathing. I've only had one asthma attack but it was terrifying, not being able to suck in any air. And yet, you lived through it, and wanted your corn muffin and to watch "Teletubbies" the next day.

Then there's the time I was hurrying to get you out of the tub so we could go somewhere. I stood up from kneeling and reached for something on the top shelf of the closet, and the next thing I knew, I'm lying on the floor of the closet.

"Mommy," you called.

"He brought you back," Nancy said.

But probably my favorite memory was going to get you up in the morning after I heard the crib squeaking. You were standing, holding onto the railings, with this beautiful smile that broke across your face the minute you saw me. In that moment, I was your mother.

You're only three months old when the planes crash into the towers. I'm waiting for the babysitter so I can go out and be free. I have the "Today Show" on and suddenly, a reporter breaks in and says a plane has ripped through one of the twin towers.

At first, I thought it was just a terrible accident and as a former reporter, God forgive me, I was somewhat disappointed. What about something more exciting?

Clare arrives and I tell her Phillip is sleeping, I just fed him an hour ago, and I get in the car and turn on the radio. And instead of Luther Vandross and Stevie Wonder, it's a voice talking about the plane crash. Now it seems it may not have been an accident.

Then another voice breaks in. "There's another plane."

"No," says the first voice. "It's just a replay."

"No, it's not," says the second voice. "There's another plane." It's starting to become possible that something really bad is happening.

I continue driving and doing my errands. I can't remember now what they were, surely trivial, going to the grocery store, getting library books, having lunch. But the reports are coming in and we now know, of course, that our lives are changed forever.

I'm in the toy store when the chatter begins.

"Can you believe it?" says the cashier. "How did this

happen? And in America?"

I think of Phillip, at home. Suddenly, I don't feel safe anymore. It's such a beautiful day, bright blue sky in late summer. How can this be happening?

Some of the mortality counts are coming in as I drive home. I can't wait to get home to my baby.

I pay Clare and take Phillip into my arms. He's at an age now where he smiles when he sees me and I hold on to his warm flesh and smell him, that baby smell. Right now, I feel okay.

I just want to hold you, to feel your tiny body in my arms. So much death. And this is life. I hold you for most of the rest of the day. I stir the pasta with one hand and pick up your pillow with you under my arm. I just don't want to let go.

22

I don't remember much more about that night. Larry is working late, and we don't talk until the morning when neither of us can believe this happened.

"I'm a little scared to go back to New York," he says. "Now they're talking about the bridges being attacked."

We're supposed to go to Syracuse this weekend to see my former college roommates, who want to meet Phillip. We decide to go. Phillip hates the car. He screams every time he's in it. I dread the long trip. I sit with him in the back, at times pulling him onto my lap, and, amazingly, he calms down. I put him back in his car seat and we finish the drive.

We check into our motel; we got a suite and a crib so Phillip will hopefully not wake us. I'm still trying to make sense of all this. I don't like that he's in another room (there wasn't enough room in ours for the crib).

I take Phillip down to the lobby and it's on every TV. The planes crashing, the blood-red fireballs, the billowing white clouds of smoke and debris. For the first time I think, what have we brought him into?

There's a stillness everywhere. People talk in low voices and make sure they hold the door for others. Coming in the door, a lady looking at Phillip, says, "He's the hope of the future."

The weekend is fun, but we can't stop talking about what has happened. Jenn's grown children are there and her daughter, a teenager, is delighted to have a baby to play with. We have dinner at home the first night, then go out for dinner the second night. The restaurant is quiet, too, but we're laughing because we haven't seen each other in such a long time, and we're having fun. But no one can forget what has happened. I think we're all still expecting another flash news bulletin that something else awful has happened.

We go back home and things go a little back to normal. I still get up with Phillip at night. I have to fight with him to get him to eat his baby food, especially spinach. At least he's stopped screaming in the car.

It's Larry who continues with 9/11. He has to provide dental records to help identify the remains of firefighters who died. A friend, a firefighter, off for the day, heard the call on the golf course and raced back into New York. He's one of the last in, and he doesn't make it out. Larry is the one who identifies him.

I know life is fragile and terrible things happen, but it's unbearable, now that you are here. It all makes me think about what life would be like without you if something happened to you. It is the first time I've thought the unthinkable. That's what this has done for me. And, it's dramatic for sure, but I don't know if I could live.

23

What drew me to your father was the vulnerable child inside his raging, angry self. He has softened since you were born. He helps patients who can't speak English, even though he doesn't speak Spanish, working patiently to see if he can use words they might understand.

I've even seen him try to help some who are struggling for money. He gives directions to his Queens office carefully, adding landmarks to help, because it can be confusing, and he spends a lot of time with patients who are frightened or unsure about what needs to be done in their mouths. He doesn't sleep well the night before he goes to the dentist and this has made him compassionate and understanding.

I liked your father's decency right from the start. Your biological mother has it, too. It's clear on the donor form.

This is someone I need to love and care for all my life. But right now, I just feel like the caretaker. What is this little baby doing in my home?

There are times when I resent you. I gave up my whole life—a great job, lunches out with friends, sleep—to have you. My life has completely changed. It's repetitive and exhausting and I'm not getting anything in exchange. Of course, you're only four months old and I did get a smile (or was it gas?) at six weeks. But so far, it's been very unrewarding.

No one told me how bored I would be. Or lonely. It's

astounding that even with a new baby in the house, I am lonely.

Having a child was completely outside my comfort zone. I had no script for it at all. I saw the women pushing strollers, and smugly shielding their babies to breastfeed, as people from another planet. Suddenly, I am one of them and I'm not sure I like it.

I may still not feel like your mother, but I am certainly feeling motherhood. I'm knocking myself out to take care of someone with no acknowledgment that I'm doing anything that matters. Changing diapers and feeding this crying mouth with no sense of accomplishment.

A month ago, I was meeting with executives to learn about developing software and now I'm having to deal with things that smell and wait angrily for the next cry to interrupt my day. And sleep? Forget about sleep. I understand these are just a new parent's lament. Like marriage, I thought it would be much easier and more fun than it's turning out to be.

At least at work, you have people to talk to and go to lunch with. Here at home, I can't start writing or doing the laundry or even go to the bathroom before he starts crying. Of course, some moms would let you cry but I just can't.

I guess that all this, added to the stress of having to use a donor, picking a donor, then the anguish of wondering whose son you really are, has made your birth not exactly the miracle, or, at least, the immediate miracle, I thought it would be.

24

Your father goes to New York to see patients, and that's not fun. But then he gets to come home and plunk down on the couch while I make dinner. You fuss and I have to find out what it is you want while he goes off to play tennis or hang out with his sports buddies. And here I am, stuck at home with a baby who can't do much of anything, except cry when he wants something.

Larry's life is pretty much the same. It's mine that has been torn apart. What reassured me was that I was not alone in being terrified of a newborn.

There are small rewards. One afternoon, you're sleeping and I'm reading a book about pregnancy which has shocking information. While there might be a genetic tendency to develop in a particular way, there's a wide range of influences, beginning in fetal life, in the womb. They're learning that the womb does play a role in the development of a baby. And several years later, I learn that a researcher in Hong Kong discovered that tiny pieces of an unborn baby's DNA was found floating through its mother's bloodstream (New York Times, Sept. 29, 1922).

Of course, your biological mother had more to do with it than me. But it gives me some comfort to know that I, too, gave you some of who you are.

Maybe I am more than just a vessel that carried you. I've seen myself as an incubator, keeping you safe and healthy, getting all the right nutrients to you, shielding you with my body, more of a physical presence than anything else. I haven't felt a connection to you as your mother. I was just the thing that carried you.

It's still hard to look at you sometimes and not be jealous to see so much of your father in you.

"But you gave birth to him," Larry says.

I can't explain it, but this seems like so much less than having a baby, really, and more like having completely come from you.

Once, a mother at preschool said Phillip had my nose. I laughed, but it hurt. Of course, he doesn't have my nose. Or anything else of mine, except my heart.

Larry is more attached to the baby than I am. When he comes home, all he wants to do is hold Phillip and tell him how much he loves him. I'm in the background, fixing dinner or a bottle. I'm glad he's connected to this baby when he wasn't so sure he wanted one.

"What are you looking at?" he says.

"You. You really love him, don't you?"

"You taught me how," he says.

At night, he gets up with Phillip when he cries so I can sleep. He takes him for drives in the car, again, so I can sleep. He complains when I ask him to buy formula but he does. And when I'm feeling a little sad about losing my old life to this baby, he reminds me how much I wanted him.

Some of his bachelor days come back when he's not quite feeling the fatherhood.

"I'm going to play tennis now," he tells me one Sunday morning. I'd like nothing better than to go for a run or a swim, but I can't. I have this baby.

"Do you think you could come back early so I can go out?" I ask.

He looks at me with anger. "I've had this planned a long time. I can't cancel it now."

"I'm not asking you to cancel, just to give me some time."

"Not today," he says and walks out. But he does come home earlier than he planned and takes you for the rest of the day.

25

I remember back to when you were just born.

It's a cold, grey November day and I'm running to Lord & Taylor to pick up some socks for you. You've just turned three months and are no longer a "newborn." I feel kind of sad about that.

I don't put him in shoes, but I like to keep his feet warm in socks. He's home with the babysitter. My sister pulls up next to me in the parking lot.

"Hi," I say. "How are you?"

"Fine," she says.

"What are we doing for Thanksgiving?" She usually holds it at her house. It's much bigger and she's turning into a good cook.

"I'm not inviting anyone who calls my father a rapist," she says.

I feel the same twist of shame and guilt in my gut. But now it's in the place where Phillip was in my body. If there weren't something wrong with me, the abuse never would have happened. And since the abuse did happen, there is now something deeply wrong with me. I'm soiled, with a rotting hole deep inside me. How can I deserve anything, when I am so damaged inside? Certainly, not this beautiful baby. I don't let anyone get too close in case they might see. That's why I picked Larry, I think, because he never probed or went too deep.

I get back in my car and slam the door, then drive home too fast. I just want to hold Phillip, bury my nose in his neck because he will make me feel like I should be here, that I'm not too broken to be a mother.

And so, the days passed. I was busy with Phillip and happy. I'd had a baby! I didn't think about the donor too much. Right now, he was mine.

Christmas is quiet, just us, a pattern that is set for all of his childhood. I'm feeling a little depressed. Larry, being Jewish, does not observe this holiday, and Phillip, in later years, follows him. But it's hard to be too sad, with this beautiful boy.

26

I am starting to feel I can do this. I know now how to put on a diaper (I laugh when I think how I asked a man in CVS if diapers came in sizes), what to do when he's crying, and how to comfort and soothe him. When he cries, I immediately need to have him in my arms.

I give him a bath every morning. He hates when I wash his hair. He's not an infant anymore. He is becoming a toddler. He doesn't walk till he's seventeen months.

Larry's in the family room, reading the paper late one night (I'm sleeping).

He looks up and exclaims, "He's walking across the room!"

He will love telling this story for years.

Sometimes I worry that you will learn things from our marriage that you shouldn't. Will it seem normal to you, not to hug or hold hands? We do love each other but we do everything in private. I worry about Phillip never seeing us kiss or even hearing us say nice things to each other. I've learned that we have an "avoidant" attachment style. This means people who are averse to intimacy. It turns out that people with this style fare the worst, suffering from broken relationships because they really do love their partner but have trouble dealing with it. Will you grow up and think this is how relationships should go?

You're starting to talk. We're out for our daily run and you're saying something. It's fall, and the leaves are scratching under the stroller.

"What?" I say to you. I'm always talking to you. People look at me like I'm crazy but I like talking to you, even when you can't answer back. But now you say something with an "s" in it and I think it's "squirrel." Your first word.

You have trouble with some words. "Yellow" is "lellow," and then "yeldow," and we're walking in the woods when you scream, "A gardener snake!" as he slithers out from under your foot.

When you are about to turn three, there's a boy at daycare with disabilities, possibly autism.

"Everyone is mean to him," you tell me.

"Well, you be nice to him. You teach them," I say.

A couple of weeks later, I see you and Alex together, sitting under a tree, drawing with acorns in the dusty soil.

"Phillip," Alex says. It is one of the words he's learned to say this summer.

You may not have my genes, but I am molding you.

You are learning your letters in preschool and now you are drawing pictures every day, or writing letters. I find papers with "I love you," with your backward "e's", all over the house, and "I love Mom," when you get a little better at it.

Stick figures with a tall one and a smaller one.

"Mommy, that's me and you," you say. There is one of the house with you in the front yard, and someone looking out the window. "This is my house," you write. "I am looking out the window. My mom is looking out, too."

I am starting to realize you love me.

27

I am also starting to see a little of me in you. We're at CVS and
as we're checking out, a pack of Trident falls off the shelf. You
pick it up and put it back on the shelf.
"That was nice of you," I say.
"That's what you would do," you say.

You're getting your hair cut by my friend who's a stylist.
"He's just like you," she says, tilting his head back. "Don't
turn your head."

At about this age, you are discovering cartoons. Well, that's
not really true. Like many mothers, I plunked you in front of them
when I wanted to do something else, or just have some quiet time,
ever since you were a baby.

"Mommy, can we watch Thomas?" you ask and I change the
channel to "Thomas the Tank Engine." Next, I'll have to sit here
for half an hour, hearing all about Percy, Thomas' best friend, and
Charlie, the purple saddle tank engine who loves to tell jokes.

There are moments when I enjoy its quiet, peaceful
environment and how Thomas does so many kind things for his
friends. But there's only so much I can take of the British accent
and the train's honking horn, and when I think you'll be ok, I say
I have to make dinner or iron your shirt and you let me go.

Then there's "Bob the Builder." I wonder if that's where your
love of bulldozers came from (though, when we went to a fair
and a big man dressed as him came up to you, you cried in fear).

We're driving down the street and you yell, "Look, a

Komatsu!"

"What's that?" I say and point to a huge yellow machine on the side of the road.

"That's an excavator," you say. They're your favorite and you're thrilled that they are building a huge synagogue right behind our house. One Saturday, we walk over there, and even though we're not supposed to, I let you crawl in the shovel of the excavator and take pictures.

One night, Daddy comes home when we're watching Bob.

"Oh, my father loved Porky Pig," he says. "I'd ask for something at dinner and he'd say, 'H-h-here you g-g-g-o.'" (Porky Pig was a cartoon pig who stuttered.)

"That's terrible," I say.

"That's not the worst of it," he says. "He called me a fag because I didn't bring girls home."

I can't imagine growing up with this. I'm beginning to understand why it's so hard for him to love.

One day, we are watching "Little Bear" on TV, and he gets a baby sister and I ask if you ever wanted one. You say, yes, a sister that is two years older, which is kind of shocking, because you actually do have one. I start talking about our "helper" again and how you really do have a half-brother and half-sister and maybe someday we can meet them. You want to know why you haven't seen them and I explain that they live somewhere else but maybe someday, you all will meet. It's my dream. At least, right now.

28

A friend asked when I told you about the way you were conceived. When you are very small, probably about three, we are talking about how moms take care of their babies and I say, "I have something to tell you."

You look at me, your eyes are wide open.

"It's nothing bad," I say. "It's how you came to us."

I don't know if it's too soon to tell you, but I do it.

I say, "I had help having you,"

"Like when you needed Daddy to pick us up?" You're remembering when we got a flat tire and we needed him to come and get us.

"Yes, kind of like that. But this was a person. She helped me to have you. Some people might call her your real mother."

"Can I go play Legos?" you say.

I know you probably have not really got what I was saying and that we will have to have this conversation when you are older, but for right now, I feel better. I need you to know, on whatever level you can. There can be no secrets about how you came into this world.

Sometimes you ask me questions I don't really have answers to. You ask if God has children. You've also started asking about my life with Daddy before we had you.

"Was I there?" you ask when I tell you we're driving by where Daddy and I used to live. When you ask me where you were, I say you were with God, waiting to come to us.

We talk a lot about God. When you are four, you remind me that I said you came from God. You want to know how.

"Remember when I told you that we had help making you?"

Maybe this time it will make more sense to you. "Sometimes mommies can't have babies on their own and they need other mommies to help them. There's another lady out there who's kind of your mommy, too."

"Ok," you say and go outside to sit in your fort, the little room on top of your playground equipment where you go to be by yourself and be quiet. I loved this little haven when we bought the playground equipment because I thought you might want something like this. I did, as a kid.

Later that summer, you say, "Everybody dies."

I wait for a minute.

"Who told you that?" I'm thinking that maybe it came from camp when you learned about the animals.

"Yes, everyone dies," I say.

"If I stay big a long time, then I'll die?" you ask.

"Yes," I say. "But not for a very, very, very long time."

"Mommy, how many more days until you die?"

It takes my breath away for a second.

"A hundred days? A thousand?" you go on.

"I don't know, Phillip," I say. "I hope, a lot."

29

We talked a lot about God when I jogged with you in the baby jogger. You ask me what angels are. I tell you they help you when you're in trouble.

"Can we see them?"

"No," I say, "but they're always there."

"Has anyone ever seen God?"

"Yes, people in heaven."

"When will I see him?"

"Not for a long, long time," I say.

Last night, you came to me, after going to bed, with tears rolling down your cheeks, and say you don't want to die and lie under a stone because it's boring and you can't take Pridak, your new Bionicle (a Lego toy).

You get into bed with me. You snuggle up against me.

"I don't want to live when you're not here," you say.

"That won't be for a long time," I say, praying. "And you will have lots of friends and maybe even children so it will all be ok."

"Do you know what heaven is like?"

"No, not yet," I say. "Why do you want to know?"

But you are asleep, and I'm relieved because I don't really have answers to all the questions you are asking.

It's hard to believe but you're now in preschool. I'm putting you in the hands of strangers. On a scary night in the summer with the crickets bleating outside, there's an orientation meeting. The director says to all the panicked parents, "This isn't big school."

They have tiny little backpacks for you kids to take to school. We buy one and it seems very real that you are going to grow up.

I'm still very much unsure of myself as your mother. The other parents buzz around and we all talk and laugh in the early summer dark. But I remember feeling very much the outsider. I'm not his real mother. Am I really legitimate here?

In preschool, you make friends with a little girl. I take a photo of you at Thanksgiving, sitting in a chair together, your arms around each other. Jennifer becomes your best friend and I see how friendship is going to go for you. You will give your heart away. In the summer, we take her to the swim club, and she plays with you in the kiddie pool and climbs the big red treehouse next to you. You are always holding hands.

I love how your mind works. We're driving in the car and you ask, "What does God look like?" This is all very interesting (I think of the skinny, bearded man on the cross but it's too early to tell you) because neither I nor Larry are particularly religious.

We've been walking in a wooded preserve near the condo where Daddy and I once lived. I used to run through these woods dreaming of you and now here you are. We get out of the car and you take my hand. We cross the wooden bridge over the small bubbling creek.

I stop to show you a rock, on the other side, with mica all over it.

"This is called mica," I say.

"It's so sparkly," you say. You take it from me and turn it over, tracing the silvery mark. Then you put your hand back in mine. "Can I keep it?"

"Of course," I say. I love this. I know it won't be long before you will not want to do this.

I think about it a lot, but I know it's coming time for me to tell you about your other family. I decide to do it on our walk. It might be time to talk about your siblings. As we cross some small rocks across another stream, I say, "Remember how I told you another lady helped me to have you?

We talk about it a little.

"You have a brother and sister, too," I say.

I know there's a very good chance you will never meet them, but you need to know about them. I wait to see if it means anything to you, but it doesn't. You're too young. But we will talk about it more as you get older and you are probably going to want more. As a man I read about says, as someone whose father left him at age seven and then returned years later, , he needed to know who his father was, so he could know who he was.

30

Sometimes I can be so deep into mothering that I don't even think whose child you really are. But it's always there, like a toothache. Not bad enough to call the dentist, but you know it's there.

You've been talking about God again. Last night, as we were lying in your bed, getting you ready for sleep, you asked me if God made hats and books. I said God makes everything.

"Even me?"

"Especially you," I say.

I once saw a gorilla on Facebook tenderly rubbing the glass between her and a newborn. I guess we are all mothers, in the end.

The cancer comes out of nowhere.

I go for a routine mammogram and then get the dreaded call.

"We see something we want to look more closely at," the nurse says. Eighty percent of the time, the bright white spots on an X-ray are calcium, Google explains. So, I schedule an appointment for the coming week. It's Christmas time and I'm busy getting ready for the Christmas pageant at church. Phillip and I are going to be part of the townspeople.

In the doctor's waiting room, I begin talking to a pretty young woman.

"I've had breast cancer," she says confidently. "Nothing bad has ever happened to me in my life so I don't feel bad about getting it."

I think this a little odd and feel sorry for her. Breast cancer has to be one of the most terrible things that can happen to a woman.

"When they tell you, the radiologist wants to talk to you, that's when you know it's bad," she confides.

My name is called and I go back for my second mammogram. Afterward, they send me back out to the waiting room. They tell me not to leave.

"The radiologist wants to talk to you," the nurse says.

31

My heart is beating, thoughts racing through my head. I have a preschooler, it's almost Christmas, how can this be happening *now?* I wait to be called in. I remember looking at the walls of the waiting room, a calming shade of beige. There are pictures, too, landscapes of the sea in quiet shades of blue fading into purple. They are supposed to comfort you. It's not working.

Finally, I'm called in and the radiologist explains that the white spots could be cancer but he doesn't think so. He thinks he's being over-cautious but he feels I need a biopsy. One is scheduled for two weeks.

The days before the biopsy pass slowly but I'm busy with Phillip, and I'm grateful that I have a child who requires bathing and feeding and some dressing (okay, okay, you can wear your striped shirt) and getting him ready for preschool.

Late in the day, when I can't get out of it, we play Legos, and I take him running in the stroller. He asks me to read him a book and for some reason, I go to his bookcase. "Goodnight, Moon"? "Runaway Bunny"? I could read these without opening the books.

"How about something else?" I ask.

He doesn't know what he wants so I flip through his books and come to Dr. Seuss's "Did I Ever Tell You How Lucky You Are?"

We sit down on the carpet and I open the book and start reading. "When you think things are bad, when you feel sour and

blue, when you start to get mad... you should do what I do!'"
Even though I didn't remember it from all the other times I read
it, the words are striking something in me now.

He laughs at the pants-eating plants and poor Ali Sard who
has to mow the grass in his uncle's backyard, "'the faster he
mows it, the faster he grows it,'" and I think about my possible
diagnosis of cancer. Somehow, reading about all these silly things
makes me think I should "'be thankful a whole heaping lot, for
the places and people you're lucky you're not.'" There are worse
things, and I can get through this.

I most likely don't have cancer. Only twenty percent of the
time these spots are malignant, the doctor said. Pretty good odds.

I have to take Phillip with me to the needle biopsy and I also
take Irene, our dear old friend, whom Phillip loves and babysits
him. They sit out in the waiting room and I lie down on the table,
with my breast through a hole in the middle (it's so very weird).
Then the surgeon, from beneath, begins poking around with a
needle, over and over.

"I'm having some trouble finding it," she says. Later, a nurse
in the room tells me that's a good sign. That means it's small.
Finally, the surgeon decides I need a surgical biopsy, instead.

I go out and tell Irene. "I can't die," I say.

"You're not going to die," she says.

Since it's Christmastime, I can't be scheduled for several
more weeks. I remember on Christmas Day, while being intimate
with Larry as you nap, thinking, this isn't going to be so bad.
We're invited to my sister's for the first time. It is one of the best
Christmases ever.

Then it's the day of the biopsy and suddenly I'm not so sure.
We leave you with Irene and go to the hospital, where I'm poked
and prodded to find a vein for the IV, finally having it stabbed,

very painfully, into the skin on the top of my hand. I have to stop myself from saying, don't you know I might have cancer? I don't need this stress, too. Then, it's on to the operating room.

It's over a week before I get the results. I have just dropped you at preschool and am driving back from the grocery store. You can get used to just about anything and it has been four weeks since I first learned I might have cancer.

My cell phone rings, and it's the surgeon.

"Good news!" she says. "It's cancer. But it's not invasive."

And that's when it hits me that I have brought this child into the world, and I may not be here to see you grow up.

32

Over the next few weeks, I learn that, though it was non-invasive, it was grade three, the highest level before becoming invasive, meaning, it was about to spread outside the breast. I immediately worry about you getting cancer, too. Then I remember. You don't have my genes.

I have radiation for six-and-a-half weeks, which is supposed to give me "insurance" against it coming back. You are having a beach party with your preschool and I stand, watching you play on the sand and in the water with Jennifer, your best friend, then go to my radiation treatment, so grateful to have my life back.

"You have a ninety-nine percent chance of total remission," my surgeon tells Larry and me.

But the odds are not on my side. It returns, two years later, when you start kindergarten.

There's a day of orientation for all the kids, and Daddy and I ride the bus with you. We're more nervous than you are (a friend has a daughter starting college and I'm more upset than she is). Yes, you had daycare and preschool. But this is different. This is big school. You won't have someone looking out for you the whole time.

Your friends from the neighborhood are all on the bus and you chatter and make a lot of noise. Maybe this is going to be fun, but I still have a knot in my stomach. How am I going to let go of you for seven hours a day?

We get to school, and your teacher is there (we met her a

couple of days before school started). She's very nice. We visit your cubbyhole, where you'll hang your backpack and your rainbow towel with "Phillip" on it for naptime and your lunch, and we meet the girl you will be sharing it with. The teacher shows you where you'll lie for naptime. Not much is planned on this first day, it's more to get the parents to become more comfortable, and, after about an hour, we get on the bus to go home.

The first real day of school is different. I get you up early for a bath, then a quick breakfast and I pack your lunch (Goldfish crackers) in your backpack. We go to the bus and you get on and I run after it, throwing kisses, while the other moms with older kids look at me like I'm crazy. Like they didn't do it, too.

It's starting to hit. It doesn't really matter whose child you are. You're away from everything familiar, with thirty other kids, six hours a day, and no one is watching out for you. Then I get it. I'm starting to think like a mother.

I don't know what to do with the day. I feel gloriously free. I decide to go out to lunch like I used to do in the old days.

I remember back, a little sadly, to when words like "play date" and "sippy cup" were words I'd never heard. The first time a woman said "sippy cup," it occurred to me that I thought I knew all the words in the English language but these were new ones.

They're now as familiar to me as "groceries" and "packing lunch," my other chore words. I go out to lunch at one of my favorite places, the restaurant at Lord & Taylor. It's quiet and peaceful and mostly full of women lunching and I don't have to remind anyone to drink their milk or turn the TV down or get off the computer. This is so much fun and so unfamiliar.

I don't have to worry about anyone, I can just read the paper and sip my iced tea and revel in this new feeling that I am finally free. I immediately feel guilty. But it's so joyous. For the first time ever, for seven hours, I'm not the only one responsible for you.

I order my usual, a panini with chicken, and don't even worry about the calories. I'm so relaxed, I feel so good.

Then, I feel a lurch. Where's Phillip? It's like waking up from a dream and not knowing where you are. Then I remember. He's at school.

I try to fill the hours until you come home, but I'm only thinking about you and what you are doing. Napping? Counting? Learning letters? I don't know and won't and for a minute, I am so sad. What will I do with my life now that someone else is taking care of him? I was always a professional writer but it seems I've left that life behind, and without Phillip, I don't know how to fill the time.

I'm early to the bus stop. It's not going to be here for another fifteen or twenty minutes. But I can't wait to see you and feel your little body against mine, your skinny arms, and legs, your curly hair, your sweet little mouth, all the things that have been absent from my life today. I try not to think about the days that will come.

33

Finally, the bus is here. You come down the steps and I grab you; I don't care what the other kids say, and feel your warm, breathing flesh. It feels like I can never not feel you, solid and real, against me for another minute.

But, of course, I have to. We walk the short distance home. I feel so guilty for loving my time off that I take you to the beach. I have no idea why since we've never done that before. I watch as you play in the waves and I take a deep breath. I have survived your first day of school.

You're not too far out in the water, I'm pretty close, but I've never seen you do something like this, walk into the water so confidently and keep going out without me tagging along. You're the only one in the water. I have a picture of you by the sink, standing in the clear, green-tinged water, all by yourself. You're just looking out at the sound and smiling and I wonder if you're thinking about school and if it was a good day. Maybe letting go is not such a bad thing and something I can get used to.

On a bleak, cold day in March, the bus comes. I watch your friends coming down the steps, waiting for you. But there's no you.

"Aren't there more kids on the bus?" I ask as the bus driver starts to close the doors.

"Nope," she says, and I try not to panic. I run back to the house and arrive home, sweat streaking my hair.

I think about calling the school but don't want to take the

time. I try not to think about the terrifying episode of Dr. Phil that showed a man with a dog approaching a child and asking him if he wants to pet the dog and then go with him to get some ice cream. And the kid goes. I get into the car and race to school.

You're sitting there with your teacher in the office and I almost cry. Of course, you are safe. But there are so many things that are bad that could have happened to you, and this was another reminder.

"Mrs. Elumba said she'd take me home if you didn't come," you say. "But I knew you would come."

I'm so glad you know that.

"He got a twenty-four for reading," she tells me. "You're only expected to be eighteen at this point. He's going to be a great reader. But he's a wonderful student, anyway."

She keeps patting your head and saying how great you are.

I know I can't take any credit for this. I was always a "C" student. But I'm grateful, wherever it came from.

"See?" Larry says at dinner. He's stunned at our luck. "I was so worried we'd get a kid who had to stay back."

I'm doing all the things mothers do and I don't have a lot of time to think about just being your birth mother. I love you, no matter where you came from, and I'm doing the job, and you did come from my body, so maybe I do have some right to you.

Sometimes, you make me laugh.

"Who made God?" you ask. "Why don't we fall off the earth when the earth is turning upside down?"

One summer day, we're sitting in the backyard and talking about why you don't have a brother and I mention that I had two babies that died before you.

"Were they my brothers?" you ask.

94

I never found out the genders, and I regret that so much now.

Then you ask how old they would be, and it makes them so real, even though they had never really gotten started and were just a couple of cells in a tray, but were, no question, *life*. Then I realize that that's all you would be if we had just left the cells of the donor's eggs in a dish. Your biological mother created you but I gave you life.

I wonder what, or if, their mom has told her children about her decision to do this, and if she did it for others.

It's strange, and somewhat unsettling, to know that there are young adults out there that have parts of you in them, and them in you, but you will never know each other.

34

We're teaching you how to swim. You take lessons with the coach at the swim club and cry the first time he tries to make you go down the stairs. Fortunately, he's a kind man and lets you go at your own pace.

I work with you after your lessons. I'm not much of a swimmer and I don't expect you to be in the Olympics. I just want to make sure you learn enough not to drown. By the end of the summer, you're somersaulting off the side of the pool with your friends.

I love how cautious you are. In the beginning, I hated that you never wanted to ride a bike and that you didn't climb—except for the time you sliced your forehead open by shimmying up the car seat which was sitting on the couch and then slamming your face into the glass coffee table. I was very defiant as a child and so was your dad. But you get this from your dad.

He's always been very cautious. Where he's inching out carefully into traffic, I'm darting out. I'm seeing now how caution has paid off for you, and no matter where it came from, I'm glad.

I go to my six-month checkup with my new breast surgeon (my former one developed cancer, too). She takes a long time to come to us. It's dark and cold outside. I had to make a night appointment, she's so busy.

Because she's taking so long, I happen to see my file open

on her desk. I hesitate, then go over and page through it. And in my most recent pathology report, I see a notation that says there's a growth on my right breast, "probably benign." I don't like the word "probably."

I'm sitting on the scratchy table, with you beside me. Outside the window, it's so dark, like being at the bottom of the ocean where there is no light, just layers upon layers of black, and flashes of light from fish swimming by.

When she comes in, I go straight to the draw. "I see that I have a growth that's probably benign. Do I need a biopsy?"

"No," she says, pushing through the pages as if she's not even listening to me. She rushes through the exam, palpating my breasts as if she's late for an important appointment. "I don't see the need for it."

My oncologist hasn't recommended it, she says. "Though your body does know how to make cancer."

I have a five-year-old, I want to say. I don't want to die. I decide not only to get a new doctor but to demand a biopsy from the new one.

The news, as I feared, is not good

I know, right away, from the radiologist's voice on the phone, even though she doesn't say it. It turns out I have abnormal cells and these are suspicious in someone who has had cancer before. They can't be ignored.

I'm very lucky and get a well-known surgeon in Greenwich who, I'm told, people in New York come to see. She's kind and encouraging and is very sympathetic when I tell her I have a young child and want to live. She performs the biopsy.

There won't be another lumpectomy this time.

I have one more appointment before getting the final recommendation from my new surgeon. I'm sitting in the waiting area at the hospital and the nurse administrator, whose job is to help women newly diagnosed with breast cancer, comes over to me.

"Your case was discussed at our conference this morning," she says like it's some kind of reward.

I begin to prepare for the surgery. I'm given a meditation tape to listen to about healing (our house is broken into a couple of weeks later and they take my CD player and the tape!) and meet with the surgeon's nurse, who helps get women ready for mastectomies.

She explains everything I will go through, but all I'm thinking about is you and dying, and for the first time, I'm thinking, why did I use a donor to have a child? Why didn't I just give up and live a childless life? Living without you doesn't seem like much of a life. I am feeling heartbreak that I may not live to see you grow up.

35

Death, of course, is on my mind. The odds are good (although remember last time) of my becoming cancer-free after this operation. But knowing that these cells are running rampant through my body and that no one knows for sure if they can all be removed, I try to just stack the dishes in the dishwasher and listen to your stories about school and try to get you to bed before it's midnight.

You've been very anxious and not sleeping well. We take you to see a therapist because this is not like you. You tell him that you are worried I might have cancer again (I haven't told you yet). And when you are at school, you can't watch over me and make sure I don't die.

This was before Daddy had cancer, too, but I know this is because you are slowly starting to realize how much older we are than the parents of your friends, and what can happen.

Watching a movie, you say, "I hope I don't have kids. I don't want to have to love them more than I love you and Daddy."

I'm glad it's dark because I don't think I'm going to be here when you have kids, and it tears at my heart every time I think about it.

I know I have to tell you about this. You were very little the first time, only three, so I didn't have to go into it then.

You already know something, though. The night I learn I have cancer again, we go out to dinner at our favorite restaurant.

Larry is at the salad bar and we're alone at the table.

You look at me.

"Mommy, why do you look so sad?"

I cannot believe you have picked up on this.

It's really too early to tell you the whole story so I just say, "I'm a little sick."

Two days later, you ask again. It's time to tell you.

"I'm going into the hospital to have some surgery. I may have to stay several nights. Daddy will be with you."

I can see you trying to make sense of it. You're about to turn six. Six-year-olds should not have to deal with this.

"But I think I'll be okay," I say, hoping I'm not lying to you. You need to know the truth, but not the fear I am feeling.

"Will you be at the Kindergarten Follies?"

"I'll do everything I can," I say and am furious that this is all playing out at this time, four days before the play you put on with your kindergarten.

On a TV show, a few nights later, a character talks about the gift of cancer.

"You know this isn't forever."

We all know this. But cancer smacks you in the face and reminds you.

Sometimes now I wonder why I tried to have a child so late in life. Was it fair to him? I remember just after he was born, thinking, oh my God, I will be a social security recipient when he graduates from high school. I wonder if we'll live to see him marry, or, as I joke, ever see our grandchildren. But it's not funny and it's a deep wound in my heart when my friends talk about theirs, some of them as old as you. If you had been born to your biological mother, you'd have had her for many more years. But then, you wouldn't have us.

I've missed out on a lot in life, but I want to stay here, for you, Phillip.

36

One day, as my surgery edges closer, you won't take your sweater off to try on some new summer clothes. I lose it and yank the sweater over your head, catching your hair on the zipper. You cry out and I don't care, I just go into my room and close the door.

The next thing I know, a piece of paper slips under the door. It says, Deer Mom, I'm sorry for being mean.

I'm on the stretcher, waiting for my surgery for what feels like hours. Because I'm so nervous, I get up several times to use the public restroom, dragging all my poles with me. Finally, they come to get me and my mind goes blank. I can't think about what's going to happen to me. Instead, I think about the drawing Phillip made for me, before I left for the hospital, the two of us, side by side, together.

Then, I think about when we walked in the woods and it was winter. I asked him to hold my arm because I didn't want to slip. He put his hand on my back and that spooked me because that was what an adult would do, and someday soon, he would be one.

The operating room is, as always, freezing cold and I'm just in a thin paper gown. The medical staff talks among themselves (did I hear a Mets' game mentioned?). Instruments are assembled on the tray beside me and then I see the anesthesiologist at the head of the bed.

"Take deep breaths," he says.

My surgeon says something to me, right before the anesthesiologist fits the oxygen mask over my face.

"I'm sorry?" I say.

"I'm saying a prayer for you," she says.

All I can think about is the child I brought into this world, and what if I don't make it through this surgery? What if my cancer recurs again and he does not have a mother? All this hard work to bring him into the world, and then I leave.

I know Larry will be able to raise him, but again I think, the donor could have raised him for many more years.

The surgery takes six, almost seven hours, and when I finally wake up, Larry is sitting by my bed. I still have all these mechanisms on me, something on my legs that presses against them like a blood pressure cuff, then releases, and they tell me I have to have them on all night, puffing and letting go, to prevent blood clots.

I remember waking up with no breasts, just some kind of equipment under my gown. I later learned they were drains and would need to be flushed several times a day. It doesn't feel all that different, it just hurts right now. It's later when I realize I have no sensation in my nipples—because I have none—then it hits me. I have lost my breasts.

Though Phillip will never see me naked, I wonder if he ever did, would he think all women's breasts look like mine, one bigger than the other from my failed reconstruction (radiation, which damages your skin) and no nipples? I want him only ever to see healthy women's breasts.

Almost within minutes of my waking up in the recovery room, Larry says he has to go get Phillip, and because it makes sense, I let him. But I remember the woman whose husband came to the hospital right after her surgery in a tuxedo with champagne, to celebrate her new life.

I didn't know it then, I was just foggy from the anesthesia, but I remember thinking, you're leaving now when I've just had seven hours of surgery? Later that night, I realize that he hated hospitals and everything that went on there and, as I come to realize when he is diagnosed with colon cancer himself, when I felt it myself, he couldn't bear the thought of me dying.

Nurses come in all night to check my blood pressure and temperature. It's so peaceful and quiet in my private hospital room. No slamming doors or squeaky carts being wheeled down the hall (it's carpeted). It's like being in a hotel if you don't remember why you're there. I have these things on my legs, intermittent pneumatic compression devices, to prevent blood clots, and they pump up every couple of minutes, like a blood pressure cuff, then go back down. It's impossible to sleep.

I get up several times to go to the bathroom, dragging the IV poles with me. It turns out that's a good thing because they let me go home the next morning. I've been in the hospital for exactly twenty-four hours.

When I call Larry to tell him I can come home, he says, "But Phillip's playing Legos."

"I just had major surgery." I think I'm talking too loudly, a nurse going by looks in at me. But I'm really angry. What does he think it's been like, being chopped open and then having to wear these things on your legs that make noise and are so uncomfortable, plus these awful drains that will have to be emptied of blood three or four times a day?

"I know, I know. I'm sorry. I'll be there as soon as I can."

37

When he finally gets here, I'm all packed, and I'm just relieved to see him. I don't say anything else about the Legos. Months later, I find out that he was terrified of seeing me, not knowing how I would look. But it's just bandages and they're all under my shirt anyway.

I don't miss the Kindergarten Follies, which is just four days after my surgery. They let me into the auditorium early so I can sit down. I am still feeling weak and my legs are a little unsteady. I'm glad to be sitting down. I'm not a hundred percent. I just had major surgery. But this is what you do for your kids.

The show starts and the first kindergarten class starts singing. They're adorable but I'm waiting for you. The auditorium is too cold but I'm glad to be sitting, even on these scratchy seats.

Finally, your class is up and you're standing there, one foot crossed in front of the other, not doing anything. Not singing or dancing, just standing there. My heart goes out to you, my little child standing on the stage, terrified. I want to jump up and run onto the stage.

The number is over. Everyone claps. Then you and Yosenia go to sit down.

"Is that your son Yosenia is kissing?" asks a parent next to me.

"Yes," I say. Then I get it. I feel like I don't deserve this child. It's a hallmark of abuse. I thought about a lot of things while waiting for my surgery. My body has felt like a stranger all my life. Why wouldn't having a child in there not feel like that, too? I've never felt I've deserved anything in life—not a new car, a house, marriage to the man I loved. But you look back in the auditorium to find me and I feel it, such a rush of love for this mop-headed blond that maybe it's starting to not matter so much.

After the show, we all meet in the back of the school, on the big, grassy lawn. I'm feeling very weak and a teacher who has also been through this runs to get me a chair. I've only been out of the hospital for a few days and while I feel proud of my ability to be here, I also recognize that I'm not yet truly healed. Thank you, God, for my son.

I wasted so much of your childhood—and my life—worrying that people were thinking that I wasn't your mother. I was too old, you didn't look like me, you so skinny and me, well, a little overweight. You had your blue eyes and that blond curly hair, while mine is dark and straight. Now, I know that no one cared. It was only I who thought that.

A friend of Daddy's found out recently that he'd had a daughter years ago who'd looked him up on Ancestry.com. It had a happy ending, he welcomed her into his family.

"I bet your father has a child out there," I say to you. This was in the days when everyone had sex with everyone.

"Probably," you say.

"Would you like it if you had a half-brother or -sister?"

"I have one," you say.

I clench inside. I didn't know they were even in your mind.

"Would you like to meet them?"

"I don't care," you say.

I can't help wondering about the future. Right now, I'm your mom, you don't have any doubts about it. But what if someday you want to know about your other half?

38

I've taken to calling you "Mr. Jello," because every time I try to hug you or hold onto you, you slurp away.

I was really tired on Sunday night, and you started bugging me about sleeping in our bed. It had been a long weekend, and though I had promised you that you could, just every Sunday night, you'd spent two or three nights in the bed that week because of thunderstorms, falling asleep there, so I said no.

You carried on and carried on and I was truly exhausted. I started yelling at you and made you go into your bed, and ignored your sobs. Finally, I went in for a minute, and you said,, "I want the old Mommy back."

Today we gont shopping for school clothes and you are starting to hate trying on clothes. You are mad at me, just like a real teenager, and you slam doors and pout and give me the silent treatment. A nice lady at the Post Office asks you what we bought, and you won't answer her. I ams furious.

Sometimes you break my heart. One night, you ask again for a brother. I guess, after hanging out with Colby, your best friend, and his three brothers for two years, you want kids around you all the time, too, like in their house.

Then you say, "If I can't have a brother, can I have a cat?"

Uh, no. I'm allergic.

You are always coming up with these amazing things. You said the other day you'd like to die so you could actually see what God looks like.

We go to New York City on New Year's Day to see the big Christmas tree at Rockefeller Center. You aren't impressed, but then, it would have been much more exciting at night. I take pictures of us and then Daddy says, "Let's go to St. Patrick's," which he and I have done every time we've gone to New York at Christmas. So we do, and I explain to you about the candles I lit, hoping for you, and then you came.

"Which one was the candle?" you ask, and I point to one.

"Why is it already lit?" you say, and I explain that many people light these candles, for different reasons, but that will always be your candle. I light another one to thank God for you.

Sometimes, you surprise me. In the car, waiting for the bus, you ask me what a lie detector is. I say it's a machine that people use to tell if you're lying.

"So, is there really an Easter bunny?" you ask.

I think before I answer. You're still young enough to believe. What did your biological mother say when her other children asked?

"So, what Easter candy do you want?" I say, hoping to distract you.

"Jellybeans," you say.

I am seeing how quickly you are growing up. You are now eight. So we're at Lord & Taylor to buy you new pants and I find a pair that will fit you.

"Here," I say and hold them out. "Let's go to the dressing room."

We head toward the cubicles in the children's dressing room.

I hold the door open. "Come on. Try this on."

"You have to leave."

"What?"

"I'm not trying them on with you in here."

You're perfectly right. You have developed your own sense of privacy and space, and I must respect that. Mostly I do, but it makes me so sad because more and more, you are shielding your body from me, as you should. I long for the days when I bathed you and helped you dress, and all the other things moms do for babies and little kids, and now that's over.

"Well, just let me see them before you get dressed," I say, knowing him, and reluctantly close the door. Other doors are closing, too.

39

Sometimes I wonder if you are lonely and if you ever think about what it might be like to have a brother to share your room with, to stay up late at night telling scary stories to, an ally when you're mad at your parents. Sometimes you do talk about having a brother, and I wonder again what it would be like if you could truly meet your half-brother. Does this mean you are thinking about your half-siblings and wish, even if just for a moment, what it would be like to have had another child in the house?

But most of the time you tell me you're glad you don't any brothers or sisters,

Here you are, two weeks into your tenth year. In school, you used a program called Wordle, where you describe yourself in words, then lay it out in all directions and colors. You used words I would never have thought of like "patient" and "shy." I think I know you, and then you surprise me.

Today, at the bus stop, I told you an amazing thing I heard on TV last night, that all blue-eyed people are related to the same person from ten thousand years ago. You and Daddy are related to this person, but not me.

Then I said the lady who helped us have you had blue eyes and so she is related to you to and to the man, and she's more related to you than I am. You look at me like I'm a little crazy.

Then you say, "Mommy, I came from you. I'm more related to you than anyone."

You make friends easily, and that makes me happy. You will

have a family when we are gone. In fourth grade, you team up with three other boys and call yourselves "the posse." You do everything together and this lasts well into middle school.

My mother dies suddenly that same year. I had just gone to see her in the hospital and though the nurse said she was doing better, I knew she wasn't. She was fading in and out of consciousness and saying ridiculous things like Uncle Geoff was in the nurses' station making her a cup of tea when her brother has been dead for fifty years. She told me she was going to die in three days, and that's exactly when she did. I kissed her and said I will be back soon and even though she was barely conscious, she looked over at me, and said, "I love you."

And then she dies. Though we had some really bad times together, especially when she abandoned me after I told her about my father's abuse, I still loved her. Her saying "I love you," was her final gift to me.

My brother calls to tell me and it's such a shock. I just saw her a couple of hours ago, and now she's gone, and I break down. You come to me and put your arms around me. I don't think you've ever seen me cry before.

Nancy, your beloved babysitter, who helped me raise you, dies two months later. We go to see her in the hospital and she's her usual cranky self. She is so happy to see you and I am glad I have brought you, even though I wasn't sure if it would make you too upset. You're glad to see her, too, and tell her about the books you are reading. She always reads with you. We say goodbye and that we will see her soon. She dies four days later.

You get into bed with me that night and we talk about heaven and all the bad things that happen in the world like people dying.

"Is she in heaven?" you ask. "Is she with Irene?"

"We don't really know." I won't lie to you. "But maybe."

"Why did God have to make it like that?" you say.

I have worried about that so much, how we created you when we have not so many more years to live, and about the other bad things that could and do happen.

"I don't know," I say. "That's just the way it is." It stinks as an answer, but you are slowly learning that many sad things happen in life that you can't change. I hope it won't be our deaths, for a long, long time. This makes me think that if the donor were your mother, you'd have her for many more years.

You say you will give Daddy and me a hug when you see us in heaven. And then you say, again, "I hope I have you for a very long time."

40

You're very quiet today and I don't know if it's because of Nancy. It's November and she died in July, two months after Grandma, but I have an irritating habit of asking every five minutes if you're okay. She loved you so much, as much as I do. I stood up in church at her funeral and said she loved you sometimes more than I did. Everyone laughed. But that's not true. No one loves you more than me.

When I ask if anything's wrong, you say, "No."

I know that's not true, but I also know to leave it alone. Sometimes you can't fix everything for your kids. I am still learning this, and I hate it.

You're also learning about where babies come from. I mean, you pretty much know. But you come home with a brochure, angry.

"Why did we have to see this?" I can tell that you're embarrassed. I suspect you're talking about the birth scene, which I've heard is pretty graphic.

"I'm your birth mother. That means I was the one having the baby." I don't know if you've ever heard this term before. You continue looking in the cupboard for your Goldfish crackers. "But remember, you have a biological mother, too," I say.

You go into your room and close your door.

It's probably not the right time to bring this up, but I feel this is a good place to talk once again about the way you came into the world, and that it was the right way for us.

In fifth grade, you go away to Nature's Classroom for four days and three nights. You're nervous but excited. I put off packing for you, I think because it's hard for me. In a way, I'm thrilled that I will have four days (and three nights) all to myself but at the same time, I'm already feeling sad and empty. What am I going to do without you? Now I have no job. We've never been apart, except for all the sleepovers you had with Colby.

I did have two hotel stays of two nights each when you were just a baby and I was trying to get pregnant again, and then the one night in the hospital in 2007 when I had my mastectomy. This is different. This is joyful. Still, I'm sad and the hole in my heart is only going to grow bigger.

The hardest part is seeing the bus leave. We all get up early, me, you, and Daddy, to be at school by six thirty a.m. It's still dark out. When we get to school, parents and kids are clustered around on the platform. We see Michael John first and then he runs off to see someone else. We wait and wait for your best friend, Michael, but we don't see him. I start panicking. I ask Mrs. Longo what will happen if Michael doesn't come.

"It all works out," she says.

"Mom," you say, "I'm *fine*."

The rest of the posse is there, but no Michael. Then you see him, just hidden in the crowd, and the two of you climb on the bus and into the front seat, where you look so happy to be together and on your way.

A lot of moms cry. I don't. I don't know why. I almost do, when the bus pulls out. I know you're going to be fine and have such a great time. But what if he can't carry that heavy duffle bag, or figure out how to unroll the sleeping bag, or doesn't have enough socks? Then I realize, he will be ok. I have to let go.

41

You are changing in front of my eyes. Last week, an essay I wrote appeared in *The Advocate*. It was about how cancer changed my life but that it taught me to let go. In it, I said that letting go had a lot to do with loss and that one of my regrets in life was that I was not able to have a child with my own eggs.

So that night you and I go out to Luigi's.

"What did you think about that *Advocate* piece?" I say.

"It was interesting," you say. "Do I really have a brother and sister?"

"Yes, you do."

"Will I ever get to meet them?"

"Maybe someday," I say, hoping and then hoping not.

"I wish that I just came from you and Daddy, like everyone else, not a third person."

"But without her, we wouldn't have you."

Nancy's death affected you more than my mother's. That's because Nancy was around all the time when you were growing up and was a huge influence on your life. She was a crabby old thing but she loved you and the two of you understood each other on some level. Often, she understood you better than I did. You've been crying a lot, which you haven't done since you were very young.

Now, I don't know what brought this on (though it's near the anniversary of her death), but you are really crying and I feel so bad because there is nothing I can do—I can't bring her back—so I just put my arms around you and tell you it's okay to be sad. It *is* very sad that Nancy is not with us anymore and that, at such a young age, you have loved so many people you have lost. I know then, you're thinking about us.

"It's not fair," you say, and you're so right.

After a while, you say you feel better, but then you say you want me and Daddy to live fifty or sixty more years so we'll always be here, and then you say, "I wish I had a brother or sister, so I won't be alone when you're gone."

It's starting. I knew it would. You're pulling away from me. Remember when we crossed the street and you reached for my hand? Or the time I took you to Jamie's party and you wanted to go home with me, instead? Or all the nights you wanted to sleep with me because you liked having someone next to you.

I just wish you weren't so mean. I'm driving you to school and I ask, "How are your friends?"

"Fine," you say, and I remember, with a little bit of anger, how I couldn't stand the endless stories of what Colby ate for lunch and whom you sat with on the bus, and oh, did I know, Anna wore two pairs of socks to school?

Now it's a lot of grunts and rolling of the eyes. It's completely normal, it's what you're supposed to be doing and I see what it's like to be raising a normal kid. But I'd love to have back the days when I wished you could just leave me alone for *one* minute.

42

Of course, I did a lot of stupid things. I found a red streak in your diaper and raced you to the pediatrician.

"It's crayon," the nurse said, looking at me as though I were an idiot. And then I remembered you playing with them in the bathtub.

Or the time when you were in for a routine new baby check-up, and the end of your umbilical cord fell off on the floor, and at the time I was elated. You were moving on from newborn. But later I was sad because that was the last physical connection I would have with you.

That's when I get that it's not about you. It's about me. It's not that I feel like a fake mother. I feel like a fake everything. I've faked it all my life. I've always felt less than I am. I've pretended to be a confident, talented corporate writer, sitting around the cafeteria table, laughing with my girlfriends, worrying about getting my copy edited, flirting with the guys in the press room when I was a reporter, sailing on my soon-to-be-boyfriend's lobster boat. Confident and collected, yes. When what I've really felt like is a small child cringing in the dark.

I still find myself, at times, looking at you and thinking of your "other" mother. I don't feel that I have any connection to how bright you are, or how easily you make friends. But I am starting to feel more and more like I am in there somewhere. I am starting to see more of me in you.

I have lunch with a friend who's been fostering teenage boys.

"I still don't feel totally like his mother," I say.

"Why?" my friend asks.

"I'm not biologically related to him."

"You're kidding, right?"

"No," I say. "It's just how I feel."

"Well, let me tell you about some of the biological parents I know. Their kids join gangs and they don't even know it. They don't go to their kid's graduation. And if their kid gets in a fight with another gang member, it's up to the kid to figure it out."

I think about your friend who wound up stabbing the man at McDonald's. His brother was later shot to death in a gang fight. How did his mother not know her kids were in gangs?

"Stop beating yourself up," Jeff says. "You can have all the genes you want but, in the end, it's the kind of parent you are."

43

You've been very anxious, and not sleeping well. We take you to see a therapist because this is not like you. You tell him that you are worried I will get cancer again. And when you are at school, you can't watch me. You worry about us dying. This was before Daddy had cancer, too, but you know how much older we are than the other parents.

While watching a movie, you say, "I hope Daddy lives a long time."

Then you say, "I hope I don't have kids. I don't want to have to love them more than I love you and Daddy."

I'm glad it's dark because I don't think I'm going to be here when you have kids. It tears at my heart every time I think about it.

You start junior high and as the weeks go on, I grow used to you coming home from school and going straight to your room with the door closed. No more, "Colby ate bologna and a banana for lunch," or "Olivia wouldn't sit next to me on the bus." I feel so sad that I hated it when you did it. But isn't that what motherhood is? You hate each stage until it's over.

Again, we talk about the lady who helped me to have you. You ask if she has brown skin. I say she might, and blond hair and blue eyes, just like you. I tell you she might even look like you, and ask if you would like to meet her someday. You aren't that interested, but I also tell you that someday you may get to meet her children, your only siblings in the world.

Sometimes, now, I wonder if you think of the blood relatives who are out there, whom you don't know. You say you don't care but isn't that what all these people on Ancestry.com are looking for? Don't we all want to know whom we come from? And will they come looking for you?

Of course, you came from me. But it's not that simple. Part of me comes from my grandmother's kindness, calling me "Dolly," and slipping a dime, then a quarter, and finally a dollar into every new handbag I ever got, or my mother, who rarely did anything of the kind, rapping on the living room window when I was playing dolls having sex in the sandbox with friends, and I was terrified that she could see. But she just set out a bowl of M&Ms, my favorite candy, and invited me and my neighborhood friends in to eat.

This summer, I learn to say no to you. It's very hard. When you are having a tantrum because I won't let you jump on the couch or do somersaults. You won't stop so I put you in your room. Even though I go to get you after a few minutes, you won't come out. You stay in your room and scream and then cry, "Mommy, come get me."

I wonder if the donor would handle things differently. For all I know, I'm not doing it right. Sometimes, when I have to put you in your room, I go into mine and cry.

Using a donor to have a child is one of the most intimate things you can do with another person. You are sharing parts of your body, not unlike organ donation, which I'm sure has many parallels. But this is the most intimate part of a woman. Many times, when I could remove myself from the anguish I felt over not being Phillip's mother, I felt so close to this stranger I would

119

never know.

And yet, despite all my fears of not being able to call myself your mother, motherhood feels so natural—yelling at two little girls on bikes, no parents in sight, to get out of the way of the car racing toward them; telling a kid whose parents never accompanied him to the bus to get in the car when it was raining or snowing as we waited for it to come. I think maybe we all have it in us, but it's not tapped until you need it.

I always remember a doctor somewhere saying to me, "Well, we live till eighty these days so you'll be here for him," and me thinking if I can just make it till you're thirty.

You have lots of questions about God.

"What does God look like? When will I meet him? Is God lonely?"

I tell you he has lots of people in heaven to keep him company.

"Are you there?" you ask.

"Not yet," I say. "Not for a long time."

"Good," you say. "I want you here with me."

I talk to you a little more about the woman who helped us bring you into the world. I tell you again you have a half-brother and a half-sister. That's when you get a little interested.

"Could I meet them?" you say.

"Maybe someday," I say, and I hope I will do what I can when it's time.

But I have read that although I thought whatever makes you you came from our helper, it also came from the person who was pregnant with you. Both of us made you *you*.

44

Having a child is a miracle, especially for those of us who have struggled. There are many challenges for any parent raising a child but using a donor can create a spiderweb of anxiety and even fear. You don't have biological ties to him and someone else does. The door is open. With your own child, you know where he came from.

I don't really believe his biological mother will come looking for him or that he will pursue her. If you watch any of those shows where children do find their parents, after years apart, it's hard not to think it could happen to you. It's so heartwarming to see the parent and child reunited. Part of me wants her to find him, so I can know everything about him. But the other part worries she will want him in her life, and vice versa.

We're talking about a book I'm reading where a mom who adopted a baby years ago is contacted by the biological daughter she gave up in college and about how the two feel about each other, and who really belongs in the family.

"Kind of like you," I say. "You have another family, too."

You look at me like I'm smoking dope.

"For the longest time, I didn't feel like your mother."

"I never thought you weren't," you say.

Just when I thought we'd settled things for a while, you're screaming and yelling about taking a shower and refusing to go with me to a conference about middle school. When we got there, we stood outside and you yelled so loud I was afraid someone was going to call Child Protective Services. And again, last night, you pushed me until I had to hit you on the bottom. I even screamed, "I hate you!"

Which is unforgivable. But you pushed and you pushed and you pushed. I was tired and wanted to go to bed but you were dragging your feet about brushing your teeth. Then when you finally were ready, you came into my room and carried on, singing and humming when I asked you to be quiet. (It seems I *never* get to watch "The Office.") You kept it up until I blew my top, and that's when I said that I hated you.

Which, of course, I don't. But I hate how you act now. I know you're testing your limits but I'm getting really tired of it.

Yesterday, I saw a toddler in a shopping cart and she said to her mom, "I want to kiss you." It made me so sad because I don't have those days with you anymore. I don't like how I am with you anymore, but I don't know how to stop it.

45

You now wear contacts and the braces are gone and the girls are starting to notice you. Your first week of school, a girl tells you she likes you and gives you a stuffed bear at Christmas and a big red heart on Valentine's Day.

You learn in middle school that life isn't always fair. You get into an advanced math class and so does a friend, who didn't pass the placement test. His mother got him in there. We're more upset than you are when the kid gets an "A" in the class even though he never got above a "C" on a test. His mother set up extra credit work for him so he could earn that "A." You got them all the legitimate way, by studying and working very hard.

You've been playing intramural soccer in middle and high school and though you are not a star, you seem to like it. At least you don't run away from the ball now as you did in preschool. I have a picture of you running down the field, crying.

In freshman year, your team wins the championship. You have some very strong players, but you do your part to keep the ball moving. I go to every game. I'm so proud. After the championship game, I go over to your coach. He and I have talked a couple of times about you and he has respect for what you do on the field.

"Phillip loves you," I say.

"Phillip is an amazing kid," the coach says. "He's so centered."

Do you get that from us or your genes? Who cares?

Now you're really a teenager. Sulky when you don't get your way. Kind of snarky to grown-ups when they talk to you. Moody. And very demanding of my attention, which maybe isn't so much like the other teenager stuff. But shortly after that, you don't want anything to do with me. I'm already tasting the bittersweet of that.

I recently came across a study which investigated how mothers with eggs donated by others feel about motherhood as it relates to their child. I know I can't be alone in wondering, "Is this child mine?" It says that it takes mothers a long time to find their identity as mothers. How parents feel about their connection to their child can affect how they raise him.

Finally, after all this time, I'm beginning to realize that it may not really matter that I am not your biological mother and that my feelings, quite naturally, are rooted in the lack of a genetic tie to you.

In many cases, like ours, the child resembles the father and that can also contribute to a mother's feelings of loss and disconnection. Several mothers, as did I, expressed sadness at not being able to see their own physical characteristics in their child.

In the end, here's what counts. Your child is your child.

46

One night over dinner, we talk about who had the worst parent.

"My father used to punch me in the leg when he was teaching me how to drive if I did something wrong," I say.

"And when I asked for them to pass something at the dinner table, my father would say, 'H-h-here you g-g-g-go,'" says Larry, who used to stutter. We were determined not to make these mistakes with you. We both have experienced the damage of destructive parenting.

I feel like I'm living with a new person. I knew you as an infant, a toddler, a teen and a college student. Now, I know you as an adult.

Sometimes I look at you and think what a great job I've done. Genes matter, of course. But it's more how you've been treated and allowed to grow. No having to make you get serious about high school so you can get into a good college. No worrying about drugs. You do have friends who smoke weed and vape, but you're not interested. (Until you go away when you're seventeen and I ask what you liked most about the trip and you say, "Getting high," the first time you smoke pot). Any mother would be so very proud of you.

For some reason, I've been thinking about looking at the form the donor filled out for prospective parents. I haven't looked at it once completely, in all these nineteen years but today something is pushing me toward reading it. I look first at the photo of you as an embryo, all little curled circles, at six weeks.

It turns out, her parents were divorced when she was three and she didn't go to college. She says that her husband was initially against this, but she told him she was giving away something she "didn't need anymore."

She's Catholic and has your blue eyes, like your dad. It's weird but she's almost exactly my height and weight. She does weights and aerobics for thirty minutes four times a week, just like me. She wants to go back to school for social work and be a crisis counselor. I volunteered at the Rape and Sexual Abuse Crisis Center in Stamford for five years.

She has a Shar Pei named Jake and two cats, Jax and Katie. She's so normal. It's almost eerie how much we are alike, almost as if you were pre-ordained to come from both of us.

I've long wondered what you get from her and it makes me sad that I'll never know. Your quiet inquisitiveness? Your maturity. Your kindness. Your refusal to see the bad in anyone, despite a birth mother who sees the opposite. Daddy and I say you were born an adult. But you are just an old soul. I knew it the first time I looked into your eyes.

We talk a lot about health at the dinner table, mainly because Daddy and I have had cancer and this makes us know we are going to die, like everyone, but maybe sooner, and we want to do everything we can to put it off as long as possible.

Here's an interesting thing: I love your dad but he's very resistant to showing caring or support when bad things happen, like cancer. He is very difficult, with lots of rules and regulations. Don't wake him when he's sleeping and stay out of the kitchen when he's in there. No holding hands in public and no saying "I love you." It embarrasses him.

And yet, I love him. When he looks at me a certain way or bumps me on the hip in the kitchen, I feel a little thrill, like in the old days. In those rare moments when he's not pretending to play the violin as I say something sentimental or doing something else obnoxious, I know that, as difficult as he is, I could not be with anyone else. And I could not have made you, without him.

47

Daddy's not big on holidays and birthdays. If he never got a present, it wouldn't bother him a bit. I live for these things. One Christmas, when you are about four, you notice I haven't unwrapped any gifts.

"Mommy, you didn't get any," you say. You go to your room while I continue cleaning up. Then you come back and say, "Here." You hand me a piece of typing paper folded into a cup with a heart on it.

I worry that you may follow in your father's footsteps. Now, a lot of the time, you don't want to hug or kiss me. I get it. You're growing up. (Sometimes, out of the blue, though, you say, "I love you.")

I remember the most heart-breaking part of David Lynch's "The Elephant Man," was where the mob chases this poor, disfigured man into a corner with brooms and bats, and he says, "I'm not a monster. I'm a human being." We watched it together, and afterward, you said you'd never cried so much at a movie. This was when you saw it with friends.

Last night at dinner, your father brings up kidney stones, of which I've had three. I've been very lucky, I've never had an attack. I remember my father driving off the road on the way to the hospital when he was having one. But I've had numerous, unpleasant procedures to try to break them up. One was so big that it was blocking my kidney.

"I hope I never get one," you say, with a little fear in your voice, and I remind you that they're hereditary and since you don't have my genes, and your dad's family hasn't had them, it's unlikely. But that gets me thinking, again, about all the things we don't know about your health background and what else could be hiding there.

On a TV show, a man shows off his newborn son to a friend.

"He has your eyes," the friend says.

"Every time I look at you, I will know your eyes came from me," he says softly, looking at the baby. I will never have that.

You're starting to want more and more alone time. You go into your room and shut the door and ask me not to come in. You're not like most children with a mother who will, most likely, live a long, long time.

Our age makes me think about all the things we won't be here for. Maybe your wedding. Most likely your kids. Even reminding you to start getting colonoscopies at forty because of your father's history. Will you do it if I'm not here to remind you? I've even brought it up recently, as if, at nineteen, you're going to worry about that.

Not only are we so much older but I've had a potentially fatal disease twice now. And your father, too. I try just to live each day, not looking into the future, and though I've remained cancer-free, it's always at the back of my mind. Every once in a while, I think how much better it might have been for you if you'd had a mother who didn't have this disease.

We're sparring a lot now but then there are moments when you thank the woman who cut your hair with no prompting by me, and the Big Time Rush song you sang to me. It's all about, "I'll do anything for you, girl, twist myself upside down." Though it was weird to hear you singing those words, and I'm not sure if you know what they really mean. You are growing up. You are taller than me now.

This has been a big summer of loss for me (and you, too), but losing your love and affection, and respect, has been one of the hardest losses. I'm so sick of constantly yelling at you and telling you to apologize to me.

Now, about Larry. I mentioned early on that he wasn't so crazy about using a donor to have a baby. He's so cautious that he wouldn't agree to go to a soccer game at MetLife Stadium until he knew it had enough bathrooms. I'm more take-it-as-it-comes and at the beginning of our relationship, it wasn't a problem.

He's afraid of almost everything and that makes him uneasy about taking risks. That's why he's always hated being a dentist, he's terrified of malpractice. But you carefully eye what you want to do, and prepare for it, and only then do you do it. Does this come from your biological mother? I find myself wondering a lot more about what comes from her.

I've never thought about Larry through all this. It's been all about me. Jabbing my thigh with a needle; hoping for blood (supposedly, this means the process is working), having my hormones measured, and praying; having the devastating phone call where I learn it didn't work, or worse, that it did but it's going to end.

I've just gone through it like the soldier I am. Neither he nor I make a big deal out of anything, and I get up and go to work and come home and make dinner and life goes on. But he's been through this, too. He's been there with me, and even though he can't, or won't, talk about it, I have not gone through this alone.

I remember him asking me, when Phillip was about seven or

eight, if we should try to contact the donor and do this again. I was reluctant because I didn't think I could bear another failed cycle. We'd had three others with her eggs, after Phillip, but all had failed.

A fresh cycle was a different story. Our last three attempts had been with frozen eggs. Fresh cycles were usually more successful, though I remember a woman who was in despair because she had just found out she was pregnant with triplets, after one frozen egg cycle.

"We could do it," Larry said. "She's still young enough."

"But we're not," I said. At that point, I was fifty-four and hewas fifty-eight. Though women have done it even later, that didn't seem like the right thing for us. Or for the child.

I could see the wistfulness on his face, this man who had argued with me about using a donor, so afraid of how things could turn out. And now, acknowledging that we were past the point of becoming parents again, I saw the sadness, and I understood that this has been very hard for him too.

We would, of course, have a twenty-one-year-old or a twenty-year-old, if the pregnancies with my own eggs had been successful. The fact that we have a healthy, bright, happy nineteen-year-old is certainly a comfort. But those children will always remain unknown, and in an empty spot in my heart. I wonder, too, if this is something a donor might feel.

Even though he doesn't talk about it, Larry, too, thinks about where else our journey could have taken us.

48

It's a quiet Wednesday afternoon with not much going on.

My cell buzzes. I don't usually get too many calls, more texts than anything. I see it's my good friend Carole, so I pick up.

"Did you get that call from the school?" She's always the first with gossip. The principal had called with the news that a well-known student had killed himself and he wanted parents to know.

"Know who it was?" she says.

"No," I say, wiping the counter down, thinking, I have to cut up the lemon for iced tea and get it in the fridge so it stays cold for dinner. She says the name of a boy I grew very close to when I was teaching an afterschool course in journalism.

"He hanged himself."

I feel like I have to sit down.

"No way," I say. What's burning my throat is: you have to be kidding, he would never do that, he had so much going for him, class president, head of the student council, straight A's, lots of friends! Everyone liked this kid. Though I don't want to, I see the image his mother saw, him hanging from the shower rod.

"It must be a mistake," I finally get out.

But she says, "Nope. He's dead." She adds, "His mother found him." I can see his mother, coming home from a gala at her synagogue that night, all elated and eager to tell him about it, and opening the bathroom door, and seeing him. Neighbors said they heard the scream through their closed winter windows.

I can't get the image out of my mind

How can you love a child when something so devastating can happen? Life is full of terrible things. You can't protect your child from all of them. I had never seen the courage it takes to love a child before.

His mother is someone I have known casually through the years. When I ran into them at a synagogue, in his high school years, he gave me a big hug and a kiss.

I cannot begin to imagine this. I don't remember the rest of the conversation. I hang up and have to sit down. Phillip is in his room, playing virtual soccer with a friend. I want to go in and grab him, feel his soft skin and bony hips, his warmth, his aliveness. But I can't. I cannot think of anything worse than finding your child dead.

How do you let your child, someone you love more than life itself, out into the world where he can get hurt or sick? Or die? Rumor has it that it was drugs, but it still doesn't make sense. I know mothers have been dealing with this forever but now it's my turn. I don't know and it scares me. I don't know if I would have the courage to love a child again, something you can lose so easily.

As the Jewish religion mandates, the funeral is a day later. I get there early and the parking lot is already full. I go into the sanctuary, which is fast filling up too, and find a seat in the front row of a set of chairs toward the back.

It is mostly quiet but for some rustling and soft voices. I sit there, thinking of this young man, his curly hair, and his kindness. His father died of a brain tumor when he was ten. He bravely went on to start an annual cupcake sale to raise money for the local hospital's cancer center. How did this happen? But there are no answers and I know everyone in this room is thinking the exact same thing.

I remember talking to him about writing a piece about his elementary school days, before graduation, and what it was going to be like to leave this school, where so much of his life happened because I knew he would write about his feelings of loss and how to go on.

Over a thousand people attended. More chairs were brought in and then people just stood.

Finally, there's some sobbing in the hallway and I know it's his mother. I start crying, too, and my seat is right in front of where they pass as they head up to the front of the synagogue. I grab his mother's hand and say, "He's with you," because I believe it, and she squeezes my hand and cries harder.

I'm not a big crier but I cry all through the ceremony (a woman taps me on the shoulder and hands me a Kleenex). When it's over and I go back to my car, I feel as though my own son has died. That boy was so special to me and now he's gone. He's who I hoped Phillip would become as he grew older.

It has stayed with me all through the years (five, this year), and I have become closer to his mother. So this is what a mother is, facing the most awful of life's events and somehow, going on with life.

I think about him a lot because his mother and I have become closer friends, working together at fundraisers at my son's high school for several years. I came across a photo of him and Phillip when they were both very small and I sent it to her. She sent me back an email saying how much it meant to have me remember him, to know that other people loved him, too.

At the fundraiser, we were talking briefly about her new boyfriend, and she told me she'd dated someone for eight years after her husband's death. He wasn't the right person, but "I had to be with someone who knew my son."

So is this what a mother is? What was it like in the nights after the funeral and realizing she would have to live the whole rest of her life without him?

A neighbor's young child was stricken with leukemia at five years old. He had to go to Halloween with a helmet on his head and his mother explained that he needed to wear a mask over his face when they put him in the MRI to scan his brain for tumors.

I remember thinking how brave she was. She could be sitting somewhere and crying but instead, here she is, having a good time among the neighbors, oohing and ahhing over the pumpkins. And I thought, how can she do this? I'm getting better but I still can't stand how much risk there is in life, and you just have to take it.

49

Phillip had some bad times, too. When he was about two, I remember looking at him in the bathtub and watching his ribs go back and forth and thinking, that's weird. Then, oh my God, he can't breathe. I rushed him to the pediatrician, who diagnosed asthma and put him on prednisone, which does open his lungs, but toddlers are only supposed to have once a year.

Every time he has an attack that year, they put him back on it. I tell a friend, and she says, "You need a new doctor." I feel so guilty that I didn't know that.

Then there was the one time when he was climbing onto a baby seat from the car that was up on the couch. I saw it start to tip over with him in it, and he smashed his head against the glass table. It was like I saw it in slow motion. I saw him climbing and then the tipping and the whole time, I was thinking, no, no, no! We had to wait at the hospital, and I held my bleeding child in my lap while others were taken care of. He was so good, he never cried and just watched what was going on.

Finally, they brought him in, and he just needed one staple.

But my husband came home and said what I was afraid he would say, "How could you let this happen?"

I don't know what I would do if you had cancer, and I try not to think about it. This mother and her child stay in my mind because life is full of risks and you never know what will happen. From the beginning, I've worried about car accidents and stranger danger, though I know better than anyone that it usually happens with someone you know. And of course, illness, and I don't know at all what I would do.

Sometimes I think I've made it when I realize I'm not the only one who doesn't always know what to do.

Last weekend we watched the movie, "The Kids Are All Right," about kids who find the sperm donor who was their father. You ask me to explain it to you and I say how he was a "helper" to them like the lady who helped us.

After a minute, you say, "Will I ever meet her?" My heart kind of drops but I say yes, I would look for her if you want, but you go on to something else. It's coming, I suspect, and I have to be all right with it.

50

Sometimes, now that you are so big, we like to reminisce about when you were a baby, all the times you woke us up two or three times a night, the hours I spent rocking you and humming "Rockabye Baby," holding you on my lap, feeling the vibrations from my humming echoed in your heartbeat, the nights I went without sleep after an asthma attack and when I ran the shower and, when that didn't work, took you out into the cold. We felt lonely during those times.

Our marriage has taken some hits. During the years Phillip was a baby, we were both frightened out of our minds that we didn't know what we were doing. I remember one fight in which I took my cell with me while running because I was afraid of coming home to him.

And there's the day I will never forget. Phillip was only a couple of months old and he was in my arms. I was standing at the front door and Larry yelled something in my face. I answered back, something probably snarky, and he shoved me, me with the baby in my arms. I had never been so scared. It never happened again but it's this I sometimes remember—not watching TV with my feet in his lap as he strokes them or the time we went on vacation and were intimate three times in one day.

Larry's just a guy with a lot of baggage who never really worked anything out, and sometimes, when I see the frightened child he tries to hide, my mothering side bursts out.

Larry and I are sitting in the waiting room. I'm not worried, even though it's his first colonoscopy and he's sixty-eight. Phillip's in school and I have a good book. I'm an old pro. I've already had three, as my grandmother died of it.

"Dr. Hirsch," the nurse calls and we get up and go into a cubicle where he undresses and puts on the scratchy blue gown.

"I'm so nervous," he says.

I rub his arm. He's only had one other surgery, a hernia repair.

"It will all be fine," I say, and I believe it.

Nurses come in and listen to his heart and check his blood pressure. One comes in to insert the IV.

"I have this," she says as she pokes, looking for a vein. I see he's a little upset but she's right, she gets the needle in. He's a typical man and a terrible patient but he's also a healthcare professional. He knows all the things that could go wrong.

An orderly comes to take him to the procedure room.

"I'll see you in a while," I say. He won't let me kiss him so I touch his shoulder and say, "Remember. It's all going to be okay."

About an hour later, a nurse comes to get me as he's coming out of the recovery room. She's very kind and squeezes his hand and asks if he'd like a ginger ale and something to eat.

"Oh yes," he says, "I can always eat." To me, he says, "I'm so glad it's over.".

Then the doctor comes in. I'm thinking, I hope this doesn't take too long. It's already ruined my day. I have to go to the grocery store again because I forgot to get Larry's strawberries, and God forbid he should get them.

"We found something," the doctor says. "It's small, the size of an avocado pit."

I'm starting to understand why the nurse was so nice. She knew we were getting bad news.

The doctor says he doesn't think it's anything to worry about but it's got to be biopsied. We won't know for another couple of weeks that it's stage three and he needs chemo; it was in one lymph node. We thank him and leave. I want to be angry, this didn't have to happen if he hadn't waited so long. But I'm too scared.

Once again, I think if you had remained in the donor's family, you would not have to be facing this. Again. And I see that you are starting to see what it's like to have older parents. But there's nothing I can do about that. I still believe you're ours for a reason.

51

In the midst of all this, you want to get your driver's license and I've been driving with you. We get into the car on the day you are going to drive on a real road, the state road which we live off.

It's very busy and has lots of accidents. Already, I'm too controlling.

"Pass that car, he's going too slowly. Put your signal light on *now*. Watch out for that car pulling out!"

I think about telling you how my father taught me to drive, how he punched me in the leg every time I took too long to make a turn or didn't turn right tightly enough, calling me a stupid idiot. I just try to stay calm and not jam my foot on the floor when you need to brake. Though it's incredibly stressful, especially now. But I'm glad I have something else to think about.

It's time to tell you about Daddy.

"So, I have something I need to tell you," I say. Thinking back, it probably was not the right time to do this. But you look at me and I see a little line of worry cross your face.

"Yes?" you say.

I was lucky when I had cancer because you were really too young to understand. But now, at seventeen, you know that people die.

"Daddy may have cancer," I say and watch your face. It stays focused on the road.

"You remember I had it, too, and I'm still here," I say, trying

141

for a light touch. But it doesn't work, at least, for me.

"He's going to be fine," I say. Who knows? But I'm reassuring myself as much as I am him.

I wait, hands clenched, for your reaction.

"Okay," you say. "Can I drive on the parkway now?"

I'm trying to force down my anger that Larry waited so long for this test. I've bugged him for years. But what I really am is terrified. How are we going to get through the next five years, when he will be considered cancer-free? I guess the same way I did, one hour at a time.

"What if they can't find my vein?" Some nurses have had trouble and he's often had to demand a phlebotomist. "What if it's painful?" I know he is just working around all the little things so he doesn't have to think of the big one: Am I going to die?

"Stop," I say. "Just stop." It's mostly to comfort him, but I can't think about this, either. What will I do if it's spread too far?

He jams on his brakes as a car with bright lights heads toward us. I should be the one driving. We've always been equal partners but right now, I want him to be in charge.

We get to the hospital, and he's taken into a room and given a gown, which he puts on reluctantly.

"Was it like this for you?" he asks, and it's the first time we've ever discussed my cancer.

The nurse comes to take his temperature and his blood pressure. "You're all set," she says, and he grimaces.

Finally, they come to take him. The surgeon meets briefly with me and says it shouldn't take that long. My surgery took seven hours. I try to do some work and watch the news on the big TV screen. But all I am thinking is, this can't be it. I never thought I might have to do this without Larry.

52

I see the surgeon coming. He's smiling.

"He did great," he says. "He's in recovery."

After a while, they let me in to see him. I've never seen him this way. He is pale and gray and he is unconscious. This is serious. Now I know why he couldn't wait to leave the room after my surgery.

I don't think I've ever felt this stressed. Here we have brought this boy into the world, possibly only to lose one of the people most important to him.

The surgeon helps us pick an oncologist. Ironically, it's the one I went to. When we meet with him, I say, "Do we get a family discount?"

Nobody laughs.

"Will I lose my hair?" is Larry's first question.

"No, not with this type of chemo," Dr. Lee says. "But you'll probably have neuropathy and nausea, and definitely fatigue, but we can give you something for that."

"I don't care, as long as I don't lose my hair."

He tells us the cancer is somewhat advanced. "But you have a ninety percent chance of surviving if you can go five years."

Again, I think of Phillip. Is this God's way of saying we shouldn't have done this? Or maybe to be more grateful than ever that we have him. I never, ever thought I might have to do this without Larry.

On the way to his first chemo, he tells me, "I'm so sorry I wasn't there for you. I never knew what this was like."

The set-up is nice, with comfortable lounging chairs for the patients and doughnuts, and sandwiches with hot drinks if you aren't nauseous, and the nicest nurses on the planet.

"Is there anything I can do for you before we get started?" the nurse asks as he settles into his treatment chair and she arranges a pillow behind his neck. "We're going to do our best to make it as painless and pleasant as possible." She gives him a wry smile. "I know this is the last place you want to be but we're going to make you as comfortable as we can."

Another nurse comes into the cubicle, which is very private with wrap-around curtains. She's wheeling in the caustic chemicals which are so dangerous they have to wear thick plastic gloves to administer them. And they're putting this into my husband.

A different nurse comes and checks them over to make sure they're the right ones. He will have treatments every other week for six months.

Fortunately, Larry doesn't have the nausea that frequently accompanies this, and his biggest fear, that he will lose his hair, doesn't happen. I'm so glad for Phillip, too. This is the biggest indication that you are very sick.

57

It becomes somewhat routine after the first couple of months but every time I look at Larry's thinning face (he's lost fifty pounds), I think, why did we do this, have a child so late in life when illnesses like this are so common? Would Phillip have been better off with his biological family, so much younger, and healthier? What will he do if Larry dies? Were we right to have even started this journey to have this child?

As with my cancer, there are no answers.

I'm feeling this strange thing. I want to meet this woman, the biological mother of my child.

It's all done anonymously but the other day, I went online and tried to find a directory that might list police dispatchers from the late '90s and early 2000s. That was her job at the time. I doubt I could really get to her but I'm finding, now, that it's always in the back of my mind.

I ask you if you'd like to see the form your biological mother filled out.

"Okay," you say. "That might be interesting." And you take the documents. It makes me a little panicky. I have never considered doing it before—I think I was scared—but I think it's time to look back and as I begin reading her very neat (Catholic school?) hand-writing.

It makes me start thinking, again, about who she is, how she lives her life, and how already having two children might make it harder to give up eggs that might produce a child. I have, of course, thought about her a lot through these years. What has it been like for her to not know if there are children out there who came from her? I start to feel grateful and sad, then panic again because she has equal claim to my son.

But I'm sure I can find her. At the time, she only lived about forty miles away. And she had a municipal job so I could probably find her if I wanted.

I'm feeling this sense of wanting to meet her, to get to know every aspect of my child. Do other donor recipients want this? I'm reading a novel right now about a woman considering sperm donation but not feeling right about the child who's conceived in that way. How will that child feel about it? Will he be happy or mad?

Of course, in the end, most of me doesn't really want to, because that would make her real, though I do like looking at her neat, rounded, Catholic school handwriting. It makes me feel closer to her.

Children who come into the world through a donor very often find out by accident. Today, offspring are looking for that donor. Of course, we told Phillip when he was old enough to understand and so far, he doesn't seem to have the emptiness of these children who are missing half their story (as an author puts it).

53

I wonder how you will feel, later in life, as a donor-conceived child. Women have been receiving donor eggs since 1984. Lots has been written about the women like me seeking donors but not much about how the children conceived this way feel. That's given me something new to think about, too.

In fact, new books are being written about this. In the past, it's all been from the mother's point of view. But now women are writing about how they feel about finding out they were conceived using a donor's egg. I tell Phillip about this coming home from dinner but he says, "You are my parents."

At dinner, when you don't return the donor's papers to me, I think, you want to meet her. To know her. To have a relationship with you. She, after all, is your history.

Carefully, I ask how you feel about her.

"I don't know." You shrug. "I don't know anything about her."

"Would you like to meet her?" I ask.

"Why?" you say. "She's not my mom."

I don't know how I will feel if Phillip ends up trying to find his first family. It's taken me a long time to stop seeing her as a dark shadow hanging over my right to Phillip but as someone who has a family, as I now do, and is a mother just like me.

I had always felt her as a threat, lurking in the background. I've resented her because she could do something I couldn't. But as Phillip has grown more and more to feel like my child, she doesn't feel like so much of a competitor anymore. Maybe I'm the one who's grown.

I've always seen her as a friendly, good-natured, well-meaning young woman, someone I could be friends with, even with all the jealousy I have of her, supplying all Phillip's genes. Something has shifted in me. It happens while I am helping Phillip get ready for college. She has gone from being the donor to Phillip's biological mother.

Last night, for some reason, I bring her up again. "Do you want to talk about your biological mother?"

You shrug. "I told you, she's not my mother."

54

At dinner, we talk mostly about tennis, politics, and math. Phillip is an applied math major but as someone who got three hundred and eighty on her math SAT, I don't have a clue what they're talking about.

I'm coming in to put dinner on the table.

"You have to get used to using that left hand when you're serving, it's easy to overlook," Larry says. Is he thinking Phillip might be a competitive tennis player, too?

"Here? Like this?" Phillip asks.

"No, thumb up," Larry says. "Keep it firm as you turn it."

Here's another thing they have in common. Phillip is showing more and more interest in learning how to play and Larry demonstrates, then takes him to a public tennis court to let him try it out for himself. He's not very good. Larry's a competitive tennis player and has won many local tournaments, so it's hard for him to see Phillip so far behind.

Last night, as I I was clearing the dishes, tennis is the subject again.

"Let's go to the courts again this weekend," I said.

So, we go to a small park in an affluent suburb that has tennis nets and they begin the lesson. There's a little thrill watching Larry authoritatively take Phillip's right hand and place it on the racquet, showing him how to hold it.

"Like this?" Phillip says, and beams when Larry says, "That's right."

I see the connection between them even more deeply.

They do this for many weeks until the weather warms up.

"Now we can go to the club," Larry says, about a tennis club we belong to.

"No, not until I'm better," Phillip says, in an unusual show of being unconfident. I suspect it's because he wants Larry to be proud of him and Larry can't be when he's missing the ball.

"What about my stroke?" Phillip says.

I sit at the dinner table with them and am silent while they talk about Nadal vs. Djokovic, and the new guy who is coming up.

"What about Zverev?" Larry says.

"Or Tsitsipas?" Phillip says.

I can barely pronounce these names, let alone care how well they play tennis. But this is so important to both of them. I see how like each other they are. I love how they are with each other. I even love Larry more, seeing him with our child. He's a real father now.

They both love the same music, too, even though Phillip was not even a thought in our minds when most of this stuff came out.

We're sitting in a restaurant and a familiar melody comes over the speakers.

"Quick," Larry says. "'His parents gave him love and affection, to keep him strong, moving in the right direction.'"

"Stevie Wonder," Phillip cries, without a pause. "Living For The City!"

55

Cancer has receded in my mind and some days I don't think about it at all. But every once in a while, I'll read something, or a TV anchor will say she has breast cancer and I'll remember that I've had it twice and what my fired breast surgeon said about my body's great ability to develop this disease. Would it have been better if I had never had cancer and a bilateral mastectomy?

Sometimes I wish Phillip could have had a more normal mother.

You're a man now. We barely touch, your body is entirely off limits. I think of how I bathed you, felt your forehead for fever, stuck your foot in the pants legs, wrapped the diaper around you. Now we brush by each other in our small galley kitchen, taking care not to touch. And remembering how I could touch you anywhere, and now I'm lucky for a smile.

Yet last night after dinner, as you were going off to study, you said, "I love you."

You've been driving a lot and staying out late. We trust you so we don't say too much about it. But one night you get home at three-thirty.

"It's so late. There could be drunks on the road." I remind you about the guy I worked with who liked to come to work at five a.m. and was killed by a drunk driver.

"There are no cars on the road," you say. "You worry too much."

151

"That's the job of a mother," I say. Then I think about what I just said.

I wish your biological mother could meet this wonderful young man that we have created together. You still don't show much interest in finding her or the rest of your half-family. But I believe the day is coming, and I am getting ready. Could you be sitting next to your brother on a bus? Or could you date your sister? You hear all these horror stories about mass sperm donors, who have children everywhere, and some meet and fall in love. And what if they look for *you*?

A doctor we go to says, "This is one of the nicest young men I've ever met." Does this come from your biological mother? A lot of people say that about you. Does your good nature and kindness come from her, your decency and trying to always do what's right, no matter how hard? I'm kind of cranky so, even without my genes, you did not get this from me.

In a book I'm reading, an adopted child yearns to find his "first" mother. He thinks she will be beautiful and loving and fix all his childhood ills. I can identify with this child, but it also makes me feel a little hollow and cold inside, too.

The mother in the story tries to help him. She calls the other woman "your mother." I don't know if I would have the courage to do this.

"Will he not be our brother anymore?" asks his sister. Will he not be my son anymore? And what of his biological mother? Her life is already set with her children. What would another child do to her life? Just think. You have two kids you've known all their lives and here is another one, someone with whom you share nothing, and half of everything.

The crickets are chirping, the cicadas shrilling. You are eighteen and we're talking about the donor and you tell me I'm a risk-taker.

"I wouldn't do it," you say. "I'd need to know everything about the genes." Surprisingly, you don't seem to care about yours, the ones you don't know about. At least, right now.

As a friend suggested, I've been reading about children who had been conceived using donor eggs. Most were the results of sperm donation but I am also now hearing about those whose mothers, like me, used donor eggs. I've also heard that women who gave up their eggs may be looking for the children they conceived. And children, as I've learned, are looking for their donors.

I don't know how I feel about this. Part of me wants to meet her, to see the parts of you in her. Does she have your deep blue eyes? Your quirky smile? Your beautiful, long thin surgeon fingers? No, that's your dad's. I wish, even though I know it's genetically impossible, that you had something of mine, maybe my copper-colored eyes. Or my left-handedness? You look just like your dad. He doesn't know what a gift that is. But I'm the one who gave birth to you. And I do know what a gift that was.

A new study says almost fifty percent of donor-egg-conceived children are distressed or angry when they find out. Does Phillip ever think about this? The half of him he's missing?

"I would never take a risk like that," says my cautious child, when we talk again about his conception. "I can't believe you did that."

"I guess I just thought it would all work out," I explain. "I never knew we'd get a kid as great as you. I just trusted that we would somehow get the child we were meant to have."

I don't know if I really believed this at the time. It was just too scary to think about all the things that could go wrong, and I couldn't bear to do it.

56

Another summer night, you and I are sitting on the lounge chairs under the trees. Our annoying neighbor is mowing her lawn for the second time this week.

Over the drone of the motor, I say, "I miss my parents."

My mother died eleven years ago, and my father, last summer.

"Why? They weren't parents like you and Daddy."

"I know," I say, "but I still loved them."

"Did you forgive them?"

"No."

"So how could you love them?"

"I don't know," I say. It's a mystery to me, too. But maybe when you have a child, love kind of takes over your life.

I've made peace with my mother. I feel a resolution with her, showing her love for me at the end. Though I didn't see much of my father in the last several years, right after my mother died, I took him to outdoor concerts at my church and out for dinner because he was so lost.

Then he got a live-in caregiver and she became his family. You don't ever forget the past, but sometimes, you can forgive. Or, if not forgive, at least, try to let it go.

We were coming home from Stonybrook when I got the voicemail from my brother.

"I'm sorry to have to tell you this way but Father has died," he said.

I was sitting on the top deck by myself, Phillip and Larry

were in the covered part of the boat. The wind felt good in my hair, the sun was shining on the blue waves, and I felt nothing. I didn't know what to feel.

He collapsed at home with the caretaker and died a few minutes later. I hadn't seen him since Christmas when he was sleeping and I didn't want to wake him. Secretly, I was relieved. But now there's a moment of sorrow that I didn't get to say goodbye.

I loved my father. He was the lenient, go-to father when my mother was so remote. But my love was clouded with the shame of the abuse, so it's complicated. I was grieving, but I wasn't. It felt so strange. I went down the stairs to tell Larry on the first deck.

"You knew he wasn't going to live much longer," he said.

Age keeps coming up since my father died. We are at dinner, talking about older people having children and you say, "I wish you had me younger so you would be around longer."

I feel a familiar, deep sadness.

"Especially because we don't have any extended family," Larry says.

I tell you how your father sometimes talks about finding another donor and doing it again.

"That would be so unfair," you say.

"Murray said it wasn't fair to the child, having him at such an old age," Larry says of his uncle.

"That's why it would have been good if you had me younger," you say. "So I would have you longer. If I have a kid in fifteen years, you're going to be in your eighties." If we're even here. You don't say it, but I suspect that's what you're thinking.

This was something I worried about a lot when you were first born. Realizing that I would be sixty-five when you graduated from high school made me almost feel nauseous. The decision to have you this late sometimes makes me wonder if we really made the right choice. But I wanted you too much. Still, no matter how much I love you, it's true. It's not fair to you.

"Would you consider contacting the donor?" I ask, surprising even myself.

"No," you say, shaking your head.

57

I've learned something new about your father. We're at our second Parents' Weekend, and you're playing Spikeball. I was kind of mad because you knew we were coming, and yet, here you are, doing something else. But then I feel better because you are now more connected to school than us.

So we go out to lunch and we're talking about high school and college and, "I was in a lot of fights in high school," your father says.

"No way," I say.

"Yes, I was. I used to wind up in the principal's office all the time."

"Where were your parents?" I ask.

"They didn't care," he says.

"Were they ever called?"

"Maybe," he says. "But I never heard anything about it."

I try to think, for a moment how I could hear from the principal about Phillip and not care.

"I also shoplifted in middle school," he says.

"No way," I say again, and I look at him. It's hard to see this man doing this, with what the kind of father he is. He got up with you at two every night when you cried, so I could sleep. He drove you around in the car when you wouldn't settle down. And he walked you up and down the sidewalk at Brock's when you were a toddler so I could eat.

"I just can't believe this," I say.

"I could never do this to Phillip," he says. We both came from such darkness. But then we had you.

But I can't stop thinking about this mother. What makes her different than me? How can she feel this child is hers when he is not her blood? She didn't even give birth to him. But she is. She has raised her, and in her heart, that makes him hers.

Right before you went to college, I ask if you'd like to see the form your biological mother filled out.

"Okay," you say, "That might be interesting," and you take the documents. It makes me a little panicky, for a second, but then I think, wait. He knows you're his mother.

It makes me start thinking, again, about who she is, how she lives her life, and how already having two children might make it harder to give up eggs that might produce a child. What has it been like for her, not to know if there are children out there who came from her?

You're looking for colleges, and we've hooked you up with a friend who runs a business doing this and we work on getting his SAT scores up, which aren't bad, but which we get up to seven hundred and thirty in English and seven hundred and forty in math. I don't know why but this process is starting to make me feel like I am entitled to feel some ownership, but it does.

We spend the summer at her beautiful beachside home while she talks to Phillip about writing his essay and how he has to step up his extracurricular work. He writes his essay about having older parents.

We talk about things I haven't thought about. Does he prefer an urban college or one more out in the country? Does he want large or small? How close to home does he want to be?

She gives us a book which lists all the colleges in the

northeast and we take it home and pore through it.

"University of Maryland?" I ask.

"Too far," he says. "Maybe something in New York or Connecticut."

I'm so glad he doesn't want to be far from home. Maybe that's not good for him, but I want him close to me, where I can grab him and touch him several times a year, not just once or twice.

It's what a mother would think.

Now that you're nineteetn19, we talk a little about your biological mother. I wonder if you're the least bit curious about your other family. But I suspect there will come a time when you will want to know more about her, maybe even search for her. Writing this makes me feel a little uneasy but she is a part of your past and you have a right to it.

A close friend recently confided that his now-forty-year-old twin sons, whom he and his wife had adopted at three months, had gone looking, and found, their biological parents. He seemed uncomfortable with it and I asked how he was feeling about it.

"My wife's handling it better than I am," he said and I thought, I've finally found someone on my team.

I don't tell too many people that you came from a donor's egg. No one in my family knows but some friends do. Secrets were poisonous in my family, but I have to keep this one.

Sometimes I do wonder how we ever got so lucky. You don't do drugs. You're kind. You don't bully or even backtalk. You do your homework. You don't stay out too late, or you let us know where you are and when you'll be home (my friends have trackers for their kids). I don't worry (too much) when you have the car. I know it's all just who you are. But I suspect, now that I have the courage to read what she wrote on her form, it's also partly the innate goodness of your biological mother, whose words, now that I feel a little more confident that I might be your real mom, come through in her answers to the questions on the application form.

But I'm in there, too. And I am slowly seeing, even though I sometimes still have nagging doubts, that you are a combination of us both.

58

It's eight a.m. and the gym is stuffy and smells like dirty socks. The lights are very bright and the team, in their black t-shirts with a slash of orange, is up front, meeting with the coach.

You are running the four hundred-meter and sixteen hundred-meter, a killer. The four hundred is a cinch for you, you've run it and won many times. But the sixteen hundred, four laps around a huge gymnasium, or one mile, at the highest speed you can attain, is way beyond anything I could ever imagine. I've seen kids vomit after running it. I'm a little scared. You're scared, too. I can tell by the way you're moving your hands.

I get very nervous at these things. I think it's because I feel what you're doing as though I'm doing it, too. People say I'm too close to you, that I need to step back. But I feel every lap you take, your feet slapping the floor, the breath coming hard and raspy, the desperate need to pass this kid. And when you find the last drop of energy to spurt to the finish line, even though you're nauseous. It's like I'm in your sneakers. Would I feel this way if, somewhere deep down inside, I did not feel like your mother?

The gun cracks and I'm on my feet, screaming your name.

"Go, Phillip!" My breath is coming in gasps, like yours, and my feet are burning. There are not a lot of other parents there. I take lots of photos, searching for the perfect one, and in one, I see people on the sidelines, cheering you.

"Is that your son?" someone asks.

I hesitate. Then, "Yes," I say.

You don't win this time, and I see you're a little dejected. But you want to ride the team bus home, so I leave without you, a little disappointed. I'd love to talk over the meet with you. But you want to be with your team. I get it. Still, I wish you would want to go home with me. I realize I have to get used to this. That's what mothers do.

I'm reading a novel about motherhood, and how hard it is, when I come across this section where the author, older and a mother, tries to talk a younger woman out of donating her eggs. It's not my child, it's my egg, says the young woman. The older woman tells her she will regret it. And, of course, it's not just an egg but a possible child.

I've always been pro-choice but when I was pregnant with my own eggs, it was life, not just some cells dividing in a dish. It's the potential child that we all see in those floating eggs. Even though those pregnancies did not succeed, for the short time they were in my body, they were life. This makes me wonder how the donor might feel now if she were to see this child who her eggs produced. It's not just an egg. It's a life.

Your biological mother, though, is actually starting to recede in my life. As high school goes on, and my involvement with you gets more intense, I go for days without thinking of her. Between setting you up with help for the SAT and then driving you to take it, helping you learn to drive, and then taking you for your test (twice), I'm getting there.

You take Katy to the senior prom (a girl asked you to the junior prom and I bought you condoms because I knew she was sexually active). But Katy is a Mormon and it takes a while for her parents to agree to let you take her to the prom. It helps that you've spent Sundays at her house watching TV. You've known her since freshman year when the honors kids had all their classes together.

"She's just a friend," you say when I'm obnoxiously bugging you about how you feel about her. I see you holding hands at the beach when all the parents go to take pictures before the prom.

I have a friend, herself childless, who couldn't understand how I could not feel Phillip was my child.

"He came out of your body," she says, and it's true. But he wouldn't be here at all if someone else had not taken something from her body and given it to me. I'm tired of having to defend how I feel but always in the back of my mind is the woman who donated not just her eggs but the reality of Phillip.

There isn't time to think about whose child you are. It doesn't matter. You have to get to the end of high school and I'm helping you do it. At graduation, we get there early because your father is a little weak from his newly-diagnosed rheumatoid arthritis and the chemo.

We find a seat in the shade in the bleachers and I know approximately where you might sit, among the sea of graduates (Greg's pizza, that helps).

I am starting to know that I deserve the good things in my life. I have been raising this child for eighteen years, and while he is not biologically related to me, he's a happy well-adjusted kid who's about to graduate with honors from high school and I had everything to do with it.

59

Then the kids start massing in. I look for you but can't find you in the sea of five hundred faces. But then you take your seat and you're right in front of us with Greg, with that crazy pizza box on the top of his cap.

Your dad looks at me.

"We did good," he says.

We've never really raised you together. When you were a baby, it was all me. And now that you're older, it's all your father. We had different parenting styles. Where I worried like a crazy woman when you weren't home by three a.m., he was as calm as could be. But start talking about grades and school, and he's relentless. This is the first thing we've been able to share, and it feels good.

Then Daddy decides to go to the men's room.

"Where's the men's room?" he asks, and I point over to the stadium entrance.

"You're not going to have time," I say, thinking of the train we took to Boston many years ago and how he got off to go to the men's room about five minutes before the train was set to depart. I heard the engine revving up and he was not back. The doors were sliding closed and he squeezed in between them.

Phillip has inherited this.

"We're leaving in five minutes," I tell him, and he says, "I'm taking a shower."

Or we're leaving for the actual SAT and you're still not in

the car. I rush into the house.

"Where are you?"

"I'm coming," you say. "I can't find my sneakers."

I start to say, why didn't you look for them last night? But I stop. I hear Nancy's voice and I don't want to be that kind of mother.

"We're going to be late," I say, worried sick about the SAT (which I bombed on).

"You're always too early," he says and he's right. I have a hard time being late for anything. And on Graduation Day, it's more of the same. He and Larry are very laid-back about time, another thing they share. When we're about to leave for dinner, you'll say, "Wait. I have to take a shower first."

And now Larry's heading off to the men's room.

"You're not going to make it back."

He shrugs and keeps going. But he's not back and the graduates are massing in front of the stadium and I see he's not going to get back in time.

So I sit alone through your graduation. It's okay because I really want to enjoy this moment, how far we have come, how now you really are starting to seem like a grown-up, and something else, *mine*, and when you go up to receive your diploma, I'm crying.

I remember back to when I felt so jealous of all that you and Daddy had in common. Sometimes I felt like I was on the periphery of this family. I knew I really wasn't, but you and Daddy talking tennis, playing tennis, liking the same music. You are a miniature version of your father, and my place was in the background, especially when he started talking to you about a career and you talked about abstract algebra and statistics and applied math and it was like you were speaking a different language.

But then I think about all the time we have spent together, these last thirteen years, the elementary school years when I was worried you would get lost in a big school because you're so quiet. And then middle school, with your changing voice and growing facial hair and having to accept that I'm no longer the most important person in your life. And finally, high school, where you are coming into your own, and I can start to believe that you can handle the world on your own. All those years and you are finally starting to feel like my child.

After graduation, we all meet up (I'm only a little mad at your father), and gather with your friends. I love when you all throw your caps in the air (Greg's pizza box stays intact), and then we just stand there, joyous that we have come this far.

60

I thought I'd have you home forever, and in the early years, it almost seemed like an overwhelming eternity. But the thought of you being gone from this house, from my life, is something I never thought would arrive this fast. I thought I had forever with you, even though I knew that, of course, eventually you would go away, off to college, on to your new life.

It's hurting my chest right now to think about it. I decide to put it away.

Phillip's grades were so good that he got into the honors college at Stonybrook. They had a special ceremony to recognize the kids in July and we take the ferry over. It's hard to find parking and I am trying to acclimate myself to my son's new home, but I'm having trouble. It's only July and there's plenty of time before he's gone for good.

The ceremony Is nice. There are about one hundred freshmen in the program. I look around and wonder if any new friends are in here or maybe a girlfriend. They were. I am so very proud of you.

Afterward, there are cookies and punch and cheese and crackers. I grab a big soft chocolate chip cookie. It's delicious. We head back to the ferry. It's a beautiful day, not too hot, not a cloud in the sky. I climb to the top of the boat and sit with one or two other people. The sound of the motor is soothing. The breeze off the water is lovely. I'm feeling a little more relaxed. Maybe I can survive this.

I decide to check my voicemail. There's one message. It's from my brother.

"I really didn't want to have to tell you over the phone but Daddy died." Other than surprise—he apparently collapsed at home as his aide was making him soup and by the time the paramedics got there, he was gone—I don't feel anything. I suppose some of it is that my son is going away and another tragedy is something I just can't handle right now.

I go down the steps to the mid-deck to tell Larry.

"You knew he wasn't going to live much longer," is all he says. He was much the same way when my mother died, also unexpectedly. It's kind of what I expected, but I still feel a little sad. But I'm not sure if it's because Phillip is going to college, or because my father is gone.

It's certainly not how I felt when my mother died when it seemed the whole world was collapsing. But he was still my father, no matter how complicated our relationship was. I go back to the upper deck that's completely open, the wind blowing my hair, the calm blue water. I realize I'm in the next phase of my life, and it is all right.

My sister had arranged for a military funeral (my father fought in World War Two), with two uniformed officers folding the American flag into a triangle that they then gave to her. A bugler played Taps. I felt like I should be moved, but I wasn't.

It was strange to see all this. My sister and father had never been close. The abuse stopped right after she was born when my mother's mother moved in. But I think she loved that he gave her a reason to hate me openly.

Our animosity actually runs back years. She never forgave me for capturing my mother's rare attention in my junior year of high school. That's when I suffered from a deep depression and she was only ten. We talked for hours about how miserable I was and she resented the closeness my mother and I shared and that she couldn't be a part of. And, worst of all, she got no attention. Even though it was founded on shared abuse, which I didn't know till many years later. We were like sisters, my mother and I, in some way, under the skin.

I'm surprised I don't feel much of anything. I suspect the feelings are there but I don't want to feel them. Then I find out my father was cremated. My sister and brother decided on this. Anything having to do with the body, and my father, makes me feel queasy, even thinking of his body burning up.

After the funeral, my brother asked us to lunch. This didn't happen after my mother's funeral. Back then, I was so distraught I was pretty much in a daze. Larry, Phillip, and I went to our favorite restaurant, and I had a glass of wine. Today, we were talking about restaurants we liked, and I mentioned one near where my parents used to live and where I went often with friends. Something very tragic had happened there.

"The One Leg Restaurant," my sister says. A student from Phillip's high school lost his leg when a car rammed into the kitchen when he was working there.

"That's pretty disgusting," I said, surprising myself. I never address her. She looked startled but then she turned to her daughter and said, "I thought that was funny."

"Me, too," Stephanie said.

61

I never really made my peace with my father. Over time, I was able to be in the same room but as he grew older and more infirm, it became harder to see him as the man who had destroyed my ability to let anyone in, including my husband.

I still haven't been able to visit his grave, though he died three years ago. He's buried next to my mother, who I used to visit all the time. Now that he's there, I'm uncomfortable, thinking about it. Even after all this time, I don't know whether to hate him or feel sorry for him. He was probably abused, too. But he did so much damage to my life. I don't know if I will ever come to any feeling that isn't foggy about him.

After my lumpectomy, my brother's wife invited us all over to their home in the rolling hills of North Salem. It's a beautiful summer day and Francine has set out a tray of cheeses and glistening fruit and Rick is barbequing. The smell of grilling meat fills the backyard.

Phillip is running around with his cousin, my sister's daughter, whom he was once very close to, and whom I thought he might be able to be part of a family with, jumping off rocks and chasing and squirting each other with a water pistol. They're having a ball. Life is good.

Over dinner, my brother makes a toast to me.

"We're glad you're here," he says, raising his glass.

"Yes," my father says.

We're having dinner when nationalities come up. Your father

talks a lot about all the dentists from different countries who have come here and, regrettably, are willing to take less money from patients. He admits it's terrible for them but it has affected his own practice, too. We talk about your two Asian friends, top of the class, who did not get into any Ivy Leagues.

"What nationality was the donor?" you ask and it takes me a minute to realize you mean, *the donor*. "Wasn't she Cuban? Doesn't that make me Hispanic?" Of course, you have questions. I've just never seen you connect to your unknown identity before.

62

It's here. We are taking you to college. I'm not crying or anything but my heart feels very heavy. We've packed up all your stuff, it was so nostalgic shopping for your shower basket, though we forget the flip-flops (which you sent me a panicked text about the first week); the sheets, a laundry basket (will you really do your own laundry?). It feels so strange to realize you are using this in a home that is no longer ours.

We're taking the ferry over to your school. It's a beautiful August day, the end of summer, and the sun shines silver on the waves. I am loving the man you are becoming. But today, I feel very, very sad. I knew this was coming but now that it's here, it almost feels too hard. I know, to be a good mother, I have to be excited for you, and more importantly, let go. But it's so very difficult for me. I worked so hard to have you and now you are leaving.

I worry that you've never had a roommate and never had to share a room with anyone (except on your "guy" vacations). I wonder how that will be. The ferry docks and we drive to the campus. There are cars everywhere, unloading kids and their stuff.

I manage to get us a parking space right in front of your dorm, and then we start unloading. Each bag we bring in makes me have to fight back tears. I stop myself. You are leaving home for good. But this is good for you. It's what you have to do, no matter how it makes me feel.

I think about my friend who lost her son. How does she feel when she goes by his room? Did she keep it the way it was when he was alive, the trophies and certificates for debate team and National Honor Society, for track, or did she turn it into an office? Does she blame herself, as all mothers do, that she couldn't keep him safe? I see now that anything can happen. Phillip, thank God, isn't dying. But he is going away.

I look around the room, the bare, beige walls, the twin beds, one on either side of the room. The thin, coarse, colorless carpet underfoot. The desks, Phillip's roommate's jutting almost out into the hall. They need everything, sheets, lamps, fans. This is where Phillip will live, sharing a bathroom and shower with twenty other boys, comfortless, harsh, bare, with nothing to cushion it like pillows and soft mattresses that fit your body and the smells of dinner cooking down the hall. But this is college, I have to remind myself.

Finally, we're done unloading (your roommate hasn't shown up) and it's time for us to leave. I find I want to get out of there as quickly as I can. I can't bear to say goodbye, I've never been good at goodbyes. I usually just leave.

"Come on, let's go," I say to your father, who looks at me like he doesn't know who I am. Usually, he's got one foot out of the door the minute he enters a room. But I have to leave. I have to get out of here.

I try to kiss you, but you pull away and I get it. You are trying to say goodbye, too.

I don't remember the ferry ride home. Part of me is glad it's all over and now I can just get used to not having you home, rather than obsessing about how upset I'm going to be over losing you. I've always had a hard time saying goodbye and the thought of having to do it with you made me anxious and miserable and

173

so uncomfortable, that that's why I had to push your father to leave even before he was ready.

Would I have been so devastated if I didn't finally feel like your mother?

63

I recently read something that struck me like stepping on an electric rail. Even when your child isn't with you, he continues to exist in a part of your brain that you have to consciously work to silence, or as a low hum of anxiety that colors everything. It multiplies when they go to college.

Months later, you tell me how depressed you were when we left, because you knew no one, were all alone and felt so sad and scared. I'm so glad I didn't know this then, sitting alone in that empty room with nothing to do but play with your phone. At least, it was a nice room, on the first floor, with a tree and a huge green lawn. Your friends, which you make right away, like to knock on your window, to go let them in. All doors, as they should be, are locked. One of the first places where your mom cannot get to you. It's not like the days when I went to school and people didn't go around killing students.

In the first couple of weeks, I feel lost. I know I have to go back to my regular life so, even though I don't want to. I start up my running again and swimming at the gym and working on my writing. I try not to let the nights bring me back to the days when I was trying everything I could to get, and stay, pregnant, but I couldn't. The loss is like that, except now I have you, which almost makes it worse.

I was watching a TV show about pregnancy right after you left, and one of the experts said that, once you've carried a baby, his DNA stays in your body forever. Part of me is sorry I didn't know this when I was so tortured about being your real mother. I wonder what this might have meant to me all those years ago. But somehow now, it doesn't matter. Of course, I'm happy to have some of you in me, after all. We are connected and have always been connected, even in those dark days, and I am just realizing this now.

A few days later, I'm reading a story in the "Science Times" about what happens in the womb. Experts have found that this is the most critical part of a pregnancy because everything is determined here—which side of the baby's brain becomes the most dominant (right or left), whether he will be shy or outgoing, if he will use his right hand or his left hand, even the diseases that may be triggered later in life. So I was not just a vessel. Somehow, it's not seeming so important anymore.

I miss you most when it starts getting dark early. The nights seem so empty without the light on in your room. I could always see it from the kitchen when I was making dinner. I've never been afraid to be alone (your father works late, most nights), but now I'm feeling something I haven't felt since I met your father. I'm lonely.

But it's a different kind of loneliness. It's not the kind where you see everyone with their partners and then go home alone to your studio apartment and turn on the TV and the stereo so there will be voices filling it up a little. It's more like an emptiness that stretches inside you into one big hole.

64

I'm having lunch with my friends, which we do a couple of times a week and it's very needed now that I no longer have you in my life. Mary starts telling us about Starfish, an organization that was developed to help children from the inner city be exposed to culture that they might not otherwise experience.

"We take them to art museums and concerts and try to help them see things in life they might not otherwise be exposed to." She looks at me. "Would you like to do it?"

I think about it for a couple of days. I'm not sure it's something I'm cut out for, though I did love working with kids on their reading at my church for several years as Phillip was growing up.

"I'll call you," she says, and though I don't want to disappoint her, I'm just not sure. But as the empty days spread out in front of me, I call her and tell her I will do it.

There are several meetings where we meet the other mentors and learn about the kids in our group, and then I am given my mentee, a ten-year-old girl who lives in downtown Stamford and who rides the bus forty-five minutes to a school in the affluent suburbs.

Our first meeting is at the Government Center at the end of summer. I half-hope she won't be there. There's a young black girl with a teenager and when we all go upstairs for a meeting, I learn that she is my mentee.

I don't know what to say. She has big brown eyes and

skillfully corn-rolled hair. I decide to ask her about it. "Who did your hair?"

"My mom," she says.

"Did it take a long time?" I ask. "I have a friend who said it took eight hours."

She rolls her eyes and I feel a little better about getting to know her.

"Yes," she says.

"Well, you look beautiful," I tell her, and she does.

The meeting gets underway, and the leaders tell us all about what to expect.

I ask Sally when her birthday is.

"August fourth," she says.

"We'll have to go for ice cream," I say. "Would you like that?"

For the first time, I get a smile. It turns out the teenager is her older brother and we talk about the school system and when he graduated and then her mother comes from work. We meet and say hello but I get the sense she is wary of me.

A couple of days before Sally's birthday, I text her mom and ask if it's all right if I take her for ice cream. She says yes but when Sally comes down to the car from her high rise, another young man is with her.

"This is my brother," she says.

"I'm going to come, too," he says.

He gets in the front seat and she gets in the back, and we drive not too far to an ice cream stand. I get it. Her mother doesn't trust me. It's okay.

I ask Sally what she would like but she looks at her big brother.

"She likes the strawberry shortcake," he says, so that's what

I order for her, and I get a small vanilla cone. He says he doesn't want anything, even though I insist. It's a hot day and the ice cream is melting all over us.

I ask her if she's looking forward to going back to school after a year off because of the pandemic and she says yes. She has a very soft voice so I have a hard time hearing her and have to keep asking her what she said. I hope she doesn't mind.

The ice cream melts all over and her brother gets us more napkins. I wonder if she would mind if I brushed a little bit of strawberry off her cheek, but I don't. I talk to her brother about soccer, which he plays competitively (he and her two other older brothers were born in Africa), and it's nice. I feel like I have known them for a long time.

Then I take her home and say we'll go out again on a weekend when she's back in school.

65

I decide to take her to the Stamford Museum and Nature Center and this time, another brother joins us. It turns out he's twenty and went to high school with my son, and they were friends. This feels really good.

"I've been here before," Sally says and I wonder if I've made a mistake. But I decide to take her to the pen where the otters are, and they burst above the water for a second, then duck back under.

"Wouldn't you like to be in that water?" I say.

"Yes," she says. "I'm so hot."

Next, we walk over to the farm animals and her brother points out the goats.

"I almost got gored by one in Africa," he says.

"No way," I say.

"I was walking with some friends through a field in Senegal and there were these goats. They were all huddled up together. My friend said let's go, and I wasn't so sure but I said okay, and the next thing we know, they're rushing towards us and butting their horns into us."

"Did you get hurt?"

"Nah," he says. "But they ripped my T-shirt."

Meanwhile, Sally has gone off to look at the cows. We hurry to track her down.

"Moo," I say.

She looks at me like I'm a little crazy.

Then, we go over to where the baby goats are. We discover

that we can feed them some grass, under the fence.

"Look!" she says as one pulls a long strand from her hand. They're soft and cuddly and I know she would like to pet them.

But then someone from the museum comes over and tells us not to feed them, so we wander down again to the otter pen. I can tell she is getting bored.

"Do you want to go to the playground?" I ask.

"Yeah," she says and runs off up the big hill to the sandy ground where the slides and jungle gyms are, me following behind a little more slowly over the stones and sticks that dot the ground.

I'm so enjoying talking to her brother that for a minute, I take my eyes off her and she disappears.

"Oh my God," I say, "Where is she?"

But her brother sees her, and he goes running off to go down a huge slide with her.

"Come on the slide!" she calls to me but I tell her I'm afraid I'll get hurt. I have a habit of that, breaking my nose three times, and my wrist, twice, when I was running. I'm glad her brother's here.

She's happy to be with her brother and they climb up to the really tall slide. I'm starting to get tired, and I remember this from when Phillip was young. They want to keep going and I've about had it. I don't feel I can say anything, she's not my kid.

I take them home and don't make a date, but I know we're going to be doing a group activity with the other mentees in a couple of months.

"So how was it?" Larry says at dinner.

"I liked it," I say but part of me doesn't like the mandatory-ness of it, how I must see her at least twice a month for two hours, stay on top of her schoolwork, and make sure everything is going okay at school with her friends.

66

Our next event is birdwatching. We go to the Greenwich Audubon Center for a program by animal experts who specialize in helping injured birds recover. They have snowy owls and an eaglet and while I admit, it's a little long, it's a beautiful fall day, sitting on the grass and watching the birds swoop and fly. Sally is on her phone the whole time. But she's not my kid. I can't say anything.

"Did you like it?" I say as we get back in the car.

"It was okay," she says.

Now we go to pick up her trumpet for school. All the mentees have to play in the school orchestra and she has decided the trumpet is what she wants to play. One of her brothers plays, and he can help her.

The woman who helps out with the instruments teaches her how to hold the trumpet, and how to push down the keys. It's more complicated than it looks.

"Do you think you can do it?" I ask her.

She looks at me like I'm dumb.

"Yes," she says. I know that look.

It's the first time one of her brothers doesn't come with us.

We go up for your first Parents' Weekend, which is only a month after you've left. Daddy has to work Saturday so we actually go a day early, and we plan to spend the whole day with you. The weather is still warm enough to sit on the top deck of the ferry and I feel so happy, the wind ruffling my hair. The ferry trip is always fun, but the best part is, it's bringing us to you.

We get there and I text you. You text back that you're having lunch with your friends and can you come after that?

"Sure," I say, thinking, maybe a half-hour. But when an hour goes by and no you, I start to get a little annoyed. Your father, who gets very impatient at the slightest inconvenience, goes to take a nap in the car.

Then I see you coming with four other kids, a tall, skinny one with long hair (whom you'll room with junior year–all of the sophomore year will be spent at home taking virtual courses because of the coronavirus), and three pretty girls, one Asian, one American and one from, of all places, Bangladesh.

All I know about Bangladesh was the song, "Bangla Desh," released by George Harrison as a non-album single in July 1971, to raise awareness for the millions of refugees from the country formerly known as East Pakistan, after the 1970 Bhola cyclone and the outbreak of the Bangladesh Liberation War.

You introduce me to them and I'm so glad you've made friends, good friends, so quickly. As we're walking to your room, you say, "Shweta's my girlfriend."

"Which one was she?" I ask, immediately feeling a strange pang of anger.

"The short one with the dark hair," you say.

The one from Bangladesh. Her skin is brown and for a while, a couple of days, maybe weeks, I'm upset and it shocks me to realize I have some prejudice. I was hoping for a blond, blue-eyed girl. But then I realize how much you two care for each other. She sends you cards at home during the summer and during your school breaks that say, "Love you," and gifts for your birthday, like that T-shirt that says "Twin Peaks," your all-time favorite show, and I start loving her, too.

183

67

I try not to think about you two having sex. I know that you sleep together, somehow, in your single bed, sometimes with your roommate in the room. But that's all I know and I'm also remembering the horrible place of sex in my family.

A friend of my husband said kids spend their whole lives leaving you.

The next event with Sally is going to the library to pick out a magazine she'd like a subscription to. She decides on National Geographic and I tell her I will get her a subscription.

"Want to go for pizza?" I ask.

"Yes!" she says.

I parked on a street where there are a lot of cars going by, close to the car, and I wait until it's clear for her to get into the passenger seat. I remember this from Phillip, keeping him safe. I'm starting to feel a little something for her.

We go to the pizza restaurant.

"What do you want?"

"Garlic and tomato," she says.

We get a small one and are only able to eat three slices (me, one, and her, two).

"We'll take this home to your mom," I say.

Next, it's the Christmas play. I decide to buy her a Christmas present (the family will be in Africa for the holiday). I pick out some tiny red earrings and leave the receipt under the cotton so she can return them if she doesn't like them.

"She loved them!" her mom says to me when I tell her that.

The play is in an old historic theater and I ask if she's ever been here.

"No," she says, looking around at the statues and the grand staircase.

We go to our seats, the mentees sit in front of the mentors, and I don't like it that she's had to scoot all the way down to the end of the aisle, away from me.

The show goes on, it's a special Le Cirque show, with lots of acrobatics and amazing body feats. I check but she doesn't seem to be on her phone. Finally, it's over and we all get up. The theater is so crowded that I'm afraid I'm going to lose her.

"Don't go anywhere," I say because she's independent.

"Okay," she says.

"Do you mind if I hold your arm?" I ask. I'm really afraid to be separated from her, there are so many people. When we out to the sidewalk, it's even worse. A special outdoor event has just ended and there are people everywhere.

"I'm going to take your arm again," I say, and she lets me, and I hold her close as we make our way through the crowd.

"Hold on," I say. I can't let anything happen to her, and finally, we make our way through to the pizza restaurant where we are meeting others from the group.

It's crowded and we have to squeeze into a booth. A server puts bread on the table and I offer it to her. "Would you like a piece?"

"Yes," she says and quickly breaks off the end. "I've never had this bread."

The other people arrive, two mentors and the boys they mentor. It's crazy and noisy and crowded with people. Outside, the lights shine through on us, glittering gold and silver, with a Christmas tree just around the corner. It feels very much like Christmas. Even though she's on her phone, I give her arm a little squeeze. I like her.

We order our pizza and I ask her what she'd like to drink. They don't have her first choice and I worry they won't have what she wants.

"How about ginger ale?" I say.

"OK," she says.

I take her home and another brother comes down to get her. He waves furiously to me and I wave back. We're like family.

Sally gets out of the car and waves to me and then she goes inside. I'm feeling a weird thing. She doesn't have my genes. I didn't even give birth to her. But she feels like my child.

68

We've been very lucky. No one we know has died from the disease but no doubt about it, life at this time has become a dark tunnel where you spent the days in your room studying and taking tests instead of sitting with friends in the cafeteria or walking to class with Schweta.

You've lost a whole eighteen months of campus life and now you're back and everyone's wearing masks, and it's not at all the carefree, open life I remember when I went to college. I worry about how the death of two years of your social life, of not being able to meet with friends without worrying about whether you should meet outside in the cold or take a chance and meet in the dorm, or whether the kid coughing in the bathroom could kill you, has affected you.

Packing you up, it's not that bad this time. You do it all though, of course, you forget your pants because you've been living in shorts, and some T-shirts and your soccer shoes, which I have to FedEx to you. I still can't look at your bedroom without a pinch, knowing not will soon be empty again. Are you glad to be going back? Yes and no.

I'm not sure if you would go looking for your biological family, but what, in these days of Ancestry.com and all the TV shows about kids reuniting with their biological parents who gave them up for adoption, they come looking for you? Would they be tempted to find the sister or brother they never got to know? Did their mom even tell them? Are there other biological children out there who were also given life by their mom? What if Phillip has even more siblings out there than the two children I knew about at the time of her donation?

As you get older, you may want to find out more about his beginnings. Part of me would like to meet them, too. They are, after all, part of you. But it brings up, again, my feelings of loss that we couldn't give you a sister, or a brother to trade ghost stories with (or jump out of a closet to scare) or fight with over who gets to ride the bike first or plan to hide your father's keys so he goes crazy, furious at his absent-mindedness, until you feel bad and produce them.

Sometimes I think it would be a real tragedy if you all never got to meet. What would it be like for you to have someone close in age to you, who's related to you? Have I crippled your life, growing up without siblings, no one like you in this house, just two parents who are more the age of grandparents? What would it have been like to have a young mother, not someone like me who thinks Slum Village is a place you wouldn't want to visit, not a top ten hip hop group?

The pandemic has reshaped your college years, making some of the most important years of your young life a black hole. You lost your whole sophomore year on campus, doing remote study. You're a junior now and you've only had two full semesters on campus.

During this time, the easy familiarity with your roommate, ordering pizza at two a.m. during finals or sitting in the common room, just hanging with friends (even Screaming Ian, who shares your suite and likes to scream for some reason, but who, too, is now your friend) was not for you.

Instead of campus rallies and ordering pizza in the dorm and going to parties where there were girls, you were locked in your bedroom, staring at the walls and wondering what I was making for dinner. Your grades didn't suffer but your life as a college student did. I think sometimes about what it would have been like if I'd had to spend the first three semesters of my campus life at home. It would have been a whole different experience. And now you only have four more to go.

You did well at home, in fact, making it into the top two percent of the whole school's GPAs. So maybe it wasn't all that bad.

I guess since it's all you knew, maybe you weren't missing so much. But I think of all the interactions you could have had with teachers and your friends and other students. You'll never get that back. Life has lots of hard spots, and you're just learning early.

You're back together with your old friends, they remain your circle of friends, but you are making new ones. You really like your suitemates, even Screaming Ian (who likes to scream, no one knows why).

There was a concern early in the new year that classes would go back online because of the new variant, Omicron, which is so contagious. Since the surge, you were worried Stonybrook would revert back to remote. Even back on campus, that's the talk in the dorm.

But, thankfully, your college president says no. With the procedures they had in place last semester, all students being vaccinated and tested every other week, and no Covid infections, she says you'll stay at school. The pandemic has disrupted everyone's life. We're all waiting to go back to "normal" but the normal we're used to is never coming back.

A friend of yours who's at Yale says they're tested twice a week and can't eat in the dining halls; they have to get their food and bring it back to their rooms to eat. This is college?

At least you have a good roommate, your friend from freshman year. He even helps us move you in, along with another suitemate.

I am relaxing. You will be fine.

69

When your father calls you on Sunday nights and asks if you're happy, you say, "Yes," right away.

So, you're handling it like you've handled everything else in your life. I thought of crediting your biological mother with your poise and stability, but, in the end, it's how we raised you.

You've become so competitive—Spikeball and a ping pong tournament. You didn't win, an Asian young man, who plays the game every day and every night, did. You're not very happy.

"That's all he does, play ping pong," you say. I don't remember you being this way when you ran track.

"He gets that from you," Larry says.

I wish I knew all this before, that you don't have to have a biological child to love him. But I think I needed to go through every stage, almost like the way you go through grief. I needed to go through the anger that it was so hard to have a child with my own genes, then the denial that that could never happen, then on to the bargaining with God (please, let me keep this baby when I became pregnant the first time), and the depression that overwhelmed me when I realized this just wasn't going to happen, and finally, the acceptance. Am I here now?

This summer, I'm looking for our first ultrasound photo of you, just a blurry image of what looks like a bean, and there it is. It's hard to believe you came from this, but you did. A miracle, I think, again.

The donor says, on the form, that, after donating her eggs,

'they are no longer mine.' I am finally beginning to see that.

I remember back to that novel where the young woman so blithely admits to donating her eggs. It's so much more complicated than that.

70

I'm having lunch with friends and one starts talking about a telenovela where two women's babies are switched. They each go home with the wrong mother but don't find out for four months that this has happened.

"So what happens?" I ask, intrigued.

"Well, the mothers feel more connection to the babies they raised," my friend says. "Then they move in together so they each can be near the babies.

"One hears the baby that wasn't born to her crying in another room and her breast milk starts coming in. She gets up and goes to nurse that baby, even though it's not her genetic baby. But it's the baby she took home from the hospital and to her, it's hers."

I think about that. What made that mother feel that way? After all, the baby she gave birth to was also in the same room. I always thought the donor would feel her breast milk coming in if she saw Phillip as a baby.

"That's a little something like my situation," I say.

They look at me funny.

"I've always felt that Phillip's real mother is his biological mother." I don't tell them I always thought milk would run through her breasts if she saw him as a baby.

"That's crazy," says another friend. "You're his mother. You've raised him since birth."

"But I don't have his genes," I say.

"That's still crazy," says the same friend. They don't

understand. She, having given birth to her genetic children, feels that if he came from you, he's yours.

"What would you do if he wanted to find his biological mother?" asks a third friend.

"I'd help him," I say. "That's his right and I would never take it away from him."

"You're his real mother," says my first friend.

Driving home, I think about the telenovela some more. If that woman could do it, why can't I? That baby didn't even come out of her but she raised her as though she did, and when her biological mother wanted her back, she did not want to give her up.

I've been hearing that some children of egg donors are starting to look for their mothers and that some women who donated eggs are starting to look for the children who may have been conceived. And that siblings have been searching for siblings.

There's even a word for it now, "diblings," for the siblings of donor-conceived children.

One woman who thought she was an only child was overjoyed when she found she had a half-brother. Another man who went looking for children conceived with his sperm found a daughter and sued for custody. That's a little scary. When you have children this way, there is always an open door. I sometimes wonder how your father would feel if we had had to use donated sperm, instead of an egg.

That makes me think, again, about how we have no family who will be there for you when we are gone. Yes, you're great at making friends. But everyone needs family. How wonderful would it be for you to discover the brother and sister you really have?

I'm watching the news this morning and a story comes on about switched embryos. During the IVF procedure, the wrong embryo was implanted in the wrong mother. They find out four months into their mothering.

"Can you imagine," Gayle King says, "All that kicking, and it wasn't even yours?"

But for the parents, it's like a death.

"You go into mourning," says the father of one of the babies.

The mother wipes tears from her eyes, thinking about the baby she had to give up. That baby was her child.

71

Maybe I should be helping you find them, your "first" family. It's something that's been rattling around my head for a while. I still have days when I don't feel entitled to call you my son, but they are fewer and farther between.

Instead of feeling fear, now I am feeling, well, curiosity. Will they look like you? Will you feel an immediate spark, as one woman did whose "dibbling" found her?

I decide to watch the telenovela. Meanwhile, the washing machine is churning. I sit down in front of my computer and put the drama on. The washing machine starts heaving behind me and I know something is caught. But I can't stop watching. I feel like my life depends on it. The two characters, as different as they can be—one, a hard-charging corporate exec and the other, a quiet, troubled teenager—come up on the screen and nothing else matters as I watch this story of two mothers.

And as I start watching, my heart hurts. The two mothers bond with the baby they took home from the hospital, and when they go to the hospital to find out their babies were switched, neither wants to give up the other baby.

Larry comes home but I don't tell him what I'm doing. He has always thought I was a little nuts about this, but then, Phillip is his biological child.

The irony is, the baby's hospital bracelets were switched. My hospital bracelet is something I still have on my bedside table. When I first brought him home and saw the word "mother" on it,

I was so happy. Of course, I gave birth to him, but seeing it on the bracelet made it real.

Watching the mother cradling the baby she has known as hers in her arms, stroking the sparse hairs on her head, lifting that head to her lips, this baby that she has soothed and comforted and fed, even nursed, for four months, I get it. This baby is hers.

Something has clicked. This magical feeling I always thought the donor would have for Phillip, milk running through her breasts if she saw him as a baby, is just that. Magical. She would feel nothing more motherly toward him than this mother does to the baby who has her genes. To her, he would be a nice young man, and she would probably look at him the way this woman is looking at the baby that she gave birth to, not interested, not caring, very nice, but let me get back to my real baby.

In a later episode, when the two mothers have moved in together so each can be near their baby, one mother hears the baby she thought was hers crying, in the night, and as her breasts fill with milk, she runs to nurse this baby. It doesn't matter that this baby does not have her genes.

Maybe I should have known this all along. But I think I needed to take this journey.

72

But it all comes home to me when you enter college. I think back to your first break. I'd gotten somewhat used to you being away. But as I see you, walking down the gangplank from the ferry, the ache of wanting to touch you, to feel your skin and bones against mine, paralyzes me. My fingers are itching to touch you, to grab you by the shoulders and feel the realness of your body. It was nice texting back and forth, but this is the prize, being able to actually touch you. You're really here again.

We walk to the car and chat about your classes.

Then, you say, "My roommate keeps drugs in the room."

"What kind of drugs?"

"Cocaine and LSD. His friends say he sells them to his frat brothers."

I admit it doesn't sink in at first.

"He leaves the LSD in our refrigerator," you say, and because you don't seem bothered, I let it go. But in the morning, I jerk awake and think, *your roommate may be a drug dealer.* Even if he's not, there are illegal drugs in your room and you could be held responsible, too, if the cops got wind of it.

I call my cop friend who says, "Get him out *now.*"

I call a lawyer who says the same thing. But you don't want to move.

"Maybe he's in on it," the cop says.

But I know it's more that you hate change, that you have your routine and don't want to move to another room, and in some strange way, you like your roommate. When you go back to school, I call the dean (even though you begged me not to).

I'm petrified your roommate's going to find out you squealed but I can't take the chance. The cop told me you would be arrested, too, and thrown out of school because your roommate could say the drugs are yours or hide them in your drawers or under your bed, and you would have no defense. Even knowing about it but not reporting it implicates you.

"Where there are drugs, there are guns," the cop says.

I spend weeks in anguish after telling the school. The vice president and dean of students get involved when my lawyer sends him a letter, saying that we expect the school to keep you safe.

What if the roommate finds out? Or the kids who buy from him? They're mainly frat kids on campus but they come to the room, and though they never buy anything in the room, they talk about it. (One of his friends said, "How do you like living with a drug dealer?") The kid is never arrested, and you spend the rest of the school year together.

I've grown up too. I've realized that not being able to have a baby with my own eggs does not make me defective, or that I'm not entitled to having a baby and that's why my eggs didn't work. I'm not less than a woman who can have a child with her own DNA. I believe, even through all those heartbreaking years, that I was meant to have a child, and that that child was you.

The year moves on and the kid is never arrested, nor is your room broken into (he doesn't lock the door!) or get expelled. Like life, things happen. But still, I worry. I am responsible for you and I, as much as I can't control it, like any mother, cannot let anything bad happen to you.

That's when I know. You are my son.